MW01595579

"If you are feeling needs on the Y2K computer crisis, you will see that Mark Kellner has come up with perhaps the most concise and down-to-earth treatment of the subject. Not only is this book a very practical guide through the impending glitch, but what I especially appreciate about this approach is its sound Christian testimony. Here is proof that the Gospel is still the right answer to all of life's problems."

—D. James Kennedy, Coral Ridge Presbyterian Church

"Mark Kellner has given us a timely reference and guidebook on the whole spectrum of the millennium mania known as Y2K. His fascinating and insightful text provides both a domestic and global perspective on what we need to know and what we need to do about it—a virtual seminar on Y2K from which we all can benefit."

—Henry Gariepy, former National Literary Secretary and Editor in Chief of The Salvation Army, and author of 17 books

"Mark Kellner is our most knowledgeable contributing writer. He knows the computer industry better than anyone I know. When I want well-researched and reported stories about the world of technology, I turn to Mark Kellner because I know he'll get the job done and get it done right."

—Mark Moring, Managing Editor, *Computing Today* magazine

Mark A. Kellner

Y2K

APOCALYPSE OR OPPORTUNITY?

Harold Shaw Publishers
Wheaton, Illinois

ISBN 0-87788-942-2

Cover design by David LaPlaca
Cover photo © 1998 by Image Technologies, Inc.

Library of Congress Cataloging-in-Publication Data

Kellner, Mark A.
    Y2K : apocalypse or opportunity? / by Mark A. Kellner.
       p.   cm.
    ISBN 0-87788-942-2
    1. Year 2000 date conversion (Computer systems) I. Title.
  II. Title: Year 2000.
  QA76.76S64K45 1999
  005.1'6—dc21   98-53137
                                                CIP

03 02 01 00 99

10 9 8 7 6 5 4 3 2

To Peter and Sylvia Dalziel,
consummate communicators, masterful
musicians, and superlative servants
of Jesus Christ.

Contents

Preface: How to Use This Book   9

Acknowledgments   11

1 Countdown to What?   13

2 How Did We Get Here?   27

3 What May Happen   43

4 The Day Your Money Dies?   57

5 Planes, Trains, and Automobiles   71

6 A Millennium of Moment—or of Madness?   87

7 Quick Fixes at Church, Work, and Home   103

8 Preparing to Minister and Witness   113

9 Planning for the Home   123

10 Helping Children and the Elderly   135

11 As This Book Goes to Press . . .   141

Glossary   151

Appendix: Y2K Resources   155

Index   159

Preface: How to Use This Book

Perhaps no time in recent memory has been as challenging for Christians as is this year of 1999 on the eve of the Year 2000. This book is written to help bring understanding to the events surrounding us. It's time (maybe it's past time!) that some measure of clarity and calm is introduced into the discussion, and that's what I pray you will take away from these pages.

In the chapters that follow, you will get a glimpse of what *might* happen if the worst fears about a computer-related meltdown come to pass on January 1, 2000. You will also read about ways to prepare for potential problems at home, at work, and in your church and community.

While some of what you read here may scare you, you will find much encouragement in these pages as well. The problems posed by Y2K can be understood and managed. There is hope for everyone involved. And, as you will see in the late-breaking news reported at the end of this book, we have much to be positive about.

My purpose in presenting good news and reports of potential problems and potential triumphs is to give you the most valuable thing you can have: knowledge. If you are aware of what is happening, you can plan for your needs. I have no products to sell—you can't order food, water, or a cook stove from me—and no axe to grind. I am a reporter by training and have specialized in technology for sixteen years. I am a believer in Jesus Christ as Messiah and Lord, and my writing is informed by that relationship.

In this volume you will also read the good news about the Year 2000—news that has nothing to do with technology. Christians of every stripe and persuasion are planning to celebrate the beginning of a new millennium with rejoicing and a renewed emphasis on the One whose birth started the calendars on the march towards 2000. The chance to celebrate faith and to witness to others is the *opportunity* part of this book. You won't want to miss it.

If you read this book with an open mind, I believe you will leave it with a clear understanding of what may happen and how to deal with whatever does happen. Tell your neighbors, your pastor, your coworkers to read this book. Get the word out. Y2K is nothing to fear, especially if you are armed with knowledge.

God bless you today—and in the Year 2000.

Mark Kellner
February 1999

Acknowledgments

I am deeply grateful to many people for their help and assistance in the preparation of this book. Some played large roles, others small ones; still other good people were either inspiration before or friends after the manuscript was completed. While it might not be possible to list everyone who's helped, I would like to offer particular appreciation to:

Harold Shaw Publishers It is axiomatic that authors gripe about their publishers, but these folks are an exception. The Shaw firm is a great, dedicated team of people. Words cannot tell my appreciation for Joan Guest, editor to the stars and all-around nice person. Thanks, too, to publisher Stephen Board, marketing director Dan Stovall, publicist Laura Momary, and everyone else in Wheaton without whom this book would not be in your hands.

Christianity Today Thanks to David Neff, Michael Maudlin, Tim Morgan, and the inimitable John W. Kennedy for their assignment of a big Y2K article to me, also to Mark Moring of *Computing Today* for his Y2K assignment. Those articles were part of the inspiration (and preparation) for this book.

Compaq Computer Corp. Especially L. J. Skibbe, Diane Bolin, Ed Woodward, Hedy Baker, Julie Akstin and Simone Skretvedt of Miller/Shandwick, their public relations firm, for their help with equipment. The Compaq Presario 5630 was used extensively in the preparation and editing of this book—and it's Y2K compliant to boot!

Micron Computer Corp. Mike Rosenfelt, Joel Kocher, Tyler Andrew, Denise Smith, Rich Demaree, and a cast of thousands at their Nampa, Idaho, facility. Great people who make great products, including a Transport Trek2 notebook I have been using. Kudos, too, to Krause-Taylor Associates, which represents Micron, and a team of wonderful people from Barbara Krause and Betty Taylor to Janet McCarthy, Benjamin Gee, and Julia Carey.

Microsoft Corp. For providing Microsoft Office 2000 in Beta form for me to test and use in writing this book. Special thanks to John Duncan of Microsoft and Ann Finlay of publicity firm Waggener Edstrom on this one.

Corel Corp. For WordPerfect Office 2000, again the Beta version, but powerful enough to translate files from Microsoft Word to a format my long-suffering editor could use. Personal thanks to Dr. Michael Cowpland, Catherine Hughes, Annette MacDonald and Frank Tomei for their valued assistance.

Hewlett Packard Corp. For printing equipment, including a hard-working LaserJet 1100A printer/scanner/copier, which came in very handy during this process. A special thanks to Copithorne & Bellows's Nicole Medgin and David Sims.

Team 2000 A group of Y2K experts (and then this author) who talk and write and consult about all this. Chuck Ashman and Bob Wagman, two good friends, are key here, and I thank both for their help.

And thanks also to: Teri Robinson, Col. Henry Gariepy, Rev. Steve Hewitt, Dan Gugler, Charles Reuben, Blake Stowell, Michael P. Harden, Ph.D., Andrew O'Donnell, Stephen Lawton, David Carnoy.

Finally, particular and grateful thanks to my wife, Jean Kellner, for putting up with my marathon sessions at the keyboard while preparing this book. Thanks, sweetheart!

Chapter 1

Countdown to What?

In these hours when the world is filled with uncertainty, we have the message of hope from our Lord who has taught us to "Fear not."

Official statement, Assemblies of God

On December 8, 1998, at about 8:15 A.M., I was driving north on Highway 101 from Sunnyvale, California, into the city of San Francisco. A reporter by trade, I was en route to a news conference being sponsored by Hewlett Packard, a major computer manufacturer. The sky was a little overcast but there was no major rain, and while northern California can often seem chilly to outsiders, the weather was comfortable enough.

Suddenly, the radio station to which I was listening went silent. Nothing else seemed out of place, so I turned off the radio and continued on into town.

The scene soon changed as the car I was driving rolled down the ramp onto a city street. The first traffic light I came to was dark. Those cars headed in one direction negotiated the crossing and proceeded along the street, albeit with a bit of honking and jangled nerves.

The next intersection also had no working traffic lights. Here, too, drivers were generally courteous, act-ing as if there were a four-way stop sign. One side would advance, then another, and then the third and fourth sides, in order. At this point, I turned the radio back on and tuned to KCBS-AM, the all-news station. There, I heard the news: San Francisco, into which a million people pour each day, had suddenly suffered an electrical power blackout.

People going to work were trapped in elevators or in high-rise office buildings without essential services. A pair of window-washers on a motorized platform dangled high above the street, unable to move. Hospitals switched to back-up power, while the subways shut down. Even the city's famed cable cars ground to a halt in the face of an invisible enemy: the sudden, and at first unexplained, loss of electrical power.

I made it to that news conference, but there was no satellite link between that location and similar events in New York and London. What was supposed to be a show of high-tech razzle-dazzle became a presentation by two managers, reading from a script. The staff at the Fairmont Hotel, aided by flashlights, guided people through the hallways and made sure the public restrooms were usable.

Despite the general civility found in San Francisco that day, there were instances of problems, the most serious being the death of a seventy-eight-year-old woman, struck by a truck as she crossed a busy intersection.

Preview of the End?

All this seemed an unfortunate, but understandable happening. Within about six hours of the initial blackout, power was restored to just about every affected area. Pacific Gas and Electric, the local utility, was taking claims from people disadvantaged by the loss of power.

The whole incident was rather tame. Yet questions remained in my mind: What would have happened if the blackout had lasted through the night—such as the 1977 blackout that hit New York City, sparking looting in some sections? What if the power outage had triggered other municipal crises, as has sometimes happened in the wake of hurricanes and earthquakes? And, most of all, I wondered how long a blackout—if it occurred—might last if triggered on New Year's Day by the Y2K bug?

I was tempted to dismiss that last question as the product of an over-active imagination. Then, on a television news program that night, I saw an interview with U.S. Secretary of Energy, Bill Richardson, who was attending an event in San Jose, about sixty miles south of San Francisco. Richardson admitted that the events in San Francisco could be similar to what America faces on January 1, 2000, if the nation's power company computers don't act properly.

The suddenness of this event, the mild chaos that ensued, and the reminder that another such problem could hit San Francisco—and your town and my town— in less than thirteen months from that date hit home. Could what I had witnessed in the Bay Area that day be a preview of the end of the world?

Apocalypse When?

At almost every major calendar milestone in history since the days of Jesus, believers have expected to see his return to this earth and the institution of the kingdom of heaven, solving all of the world's problems. This return would be preceded by a time of great tribulation, some elements of which are vividly described in the twenty-fourth chapter of Matthew's Gospel, and in other prophecies throughout the Bible.

Despite Jesus' own injunction that "No one knows about that day or hour, not even the angels in heaven, nor the Son, but only the Father," (Matt. 24:36), it has long been a habit of Christians to attempt to find out just when Jesus will return. The early believers anticipated a soon-returning Christ; this much is evident from the New Testament writings. At other times, during the spread of bubonic plague in Europe or in the maelstrom of World War II, believers have even more fervently prayed, "Thy kingdom come!"

During the turbulence of the 1970s, Hal Lindsey, Pat Robertson, and others captured public attention with books claiming that time was short before the end of the world. Most recently, layman and writer Edgar C. Whisenant and Family Radio cofounder Harold Camping stirred many with chronology-based predictions of Christ's return in 1988 and 1994, respectively. Both Whisenant and Camping used various Scriptures as the basis from which they argued their date setting, as had New York farmer and Baptist preacher William Miller, who forecast a return of Christ in 1844. In the wake of the "great disappointment" which followed, some of Miller's followers founded the Adventist Church.

As the Year 2000 approaches, the second millennium after the birth of Christ takes on special significance for many believers and nonbelievers. In the Roman Catholic Church, Pope John Paul II has proclaimed a Year of Jubilee and has expressed a fervent hope to be alive to lead the church he has headed since 1978 into this new millennium. The Lutheran Church—Missouri Synod is preparing a special evangelism campaign to commence in the Year 2000, reaching friends and neighbors with the good news of the Gospel with the hope that many will be brought to faith in that year and the ten years beyond. Other denominations are planning conventions and convocations in this momentous year, while Mission America, a multi-denominational campaign, will seek to reach every American home with an evangelistic message.

For others, however, there is grave concern about what the New Year will bring. Knowing of potential technological problems, more than one individual is eyeing the turn of this century into the next with alarm and concern. Dozens of videos and books (yes, this one included) are appearing to issue a warning and to prepare people for what might happen. The Reverend Jerry Falwell, whose Liberty University and Moral Majority captured public attention in past years, is deeply concerned about what could happen.

"I plan to certainly prepare my family as I would for a forecast natural disaster; that is, water and canned goods, perhaps a generator, the simple things that most prudent people are doing," Dr. Falwell told me in a telephone interview last year.[1]

"I don't know how you would prepare for a collapsed banking and power system in this country," he continued. "Without money and transportation over an extended period, we would have an untenable situation, and I'm praying such would not be the case."

Falwell is a man of considerable accomplishment—and influence. Growing up in modest circumstances near Lynchburg, Virginia, he has built up a church into a congregation of thousands of members; created a university that has high standards (and high enrollment); and filled thousands of hours of broadcast time on television and radio with Christian preaching.

But he also caught the attention of my mother-in-law, who, worried, asked me just how serious this Year 2000 problem would be. For her, and for the millions of people around the world who are asking the same question, this book is offered to help separate fact from fiction and offer a prudent plan for preparation, whatever may happen.

Is There Anything Certain about the Year 2000?

There are two things that are absolutely certain about the Year 2000. First, barring the return of Jesus Christ before that time, it's going to happen. Second, no one can say with certainty what effects the arrival of 01/01/2000 will have on the people of this planet.

Unlike the last "turn of the millennium"—which, researchers have found, wasn't the panic-stricken time some have said it was[2]—the arrival of the next century is fraught with potential peril. This stems from something else not found on earth 1,000 years ago, and that's the widespread use of computer technology. From our VCRs to home climate systems, from the PC on your desk to the computer controlling the launch codes for nuclear missiles, there's a chip inside controlling functions.

Those chips run on software, and each chip is programmed to recognize information in a given fashion. And in the early days of computers, the amount of data a chip could handle was limited. To economize, a date such as January 1, 1960, was written as "01/01/60," which, for the past forty or fifty years, was easily recognized and understood. Just two numbers have listed subsequent years—through 1999—for the year date.

The problem will come on the first day of the Year 2000. If computers—and the software that runs them—read January 1, 2000, as the first day of 1900, problems could result. If a system believes the "new" day has already happened, a fail-safe mechanism could shut it down, or incorrect results could occur.

But that's only going to mess up the VCR or a computer game, right? Well, no. Society as a whole has some important issues to confront, and as the days draw nearer to the new millennium, you can expect to hear plenty about the potential problems and how societies are dealing with them.

Here are some of the "worst case scenarios" that have been voiced about what might happen:

- Systems which detect incoming nuclear missiles may malfunction, potentially pressuring leaders into launching "counter strikes" for an attack which hasn't happened.[3]
- The national electrical power grid could fail, shutting down electric delivery and services that depend upon electricity, such as water treatment and distribution. According to Senator Robert Bennett, R-Utah, "If our nuclear plants are not Y2K compliant and we have an interruption in the oil supply, we could see brownouts or possible blackouts in the power grid."[4]
- Without power, and with computer malfunctions, the publicly switched telephone network could collapse, meaning no 911 emergency calls and no regular communication.
- Prisons could be in danger when essential services are disrupted, leaving thousands of violent criminals in potential chaos. Locked cells may not sud-

denly spring open, but other problems could result. At California's Corcoran State Prison, home to infamous, violent criminals such as Charles Manson, only 67 percent of the "embedded systems"—devices containing computer chips—are known to be Year 2000 safe. Any prolonged failures could enrage a prison population that you wouldn't want to see upset.[5]

- Airplane crashes—the result of malfunctioning systems on board or on the ground—could strain disaster relief efforts should multiple crashes occur. Relief agencies such as The Salvation Army and the American Red Cross are already planning for this contingency.[6]

- Banks, stock brokerages, and mutual fund managers could face a mad scramble if records of accounts aren't available after the turn of the century. Already, the New York Stock Exchange has conducted contingency tests, and the Federal Reserve Bank is preparing to print between $25 billion and $50 billion in extra currency to anticipate a run on banks late in 1999. According to Federal Reserve Governor Edward W. Kelley, Jr., "We will, of course, be ready if people want to hold more cash on New Year's Eve 1999, and we will be prepared to lend whatever sums may be needed to financial institutions through the discount window under appropriate circumstances or to provide needed reserves to the banking system."[7]

These are just a few of the problems that some believe could rise up to greet us in the New Year. There's been great talk of millions of people gathering in major cities—New York, London, Paris, Berlin, and so on—to usher in this momentous event. That's all fine and good, but what would happen if the power in just one of these cities fails for a significant amount of time, say three or four days? How would these visitors fare? And how might they get back home? Or are we being silly in even asking these questions? Are these scenarios just the product of mass hysteria?

The Real Problem

Perhaps the greatest problem we face right now, relative to Y2K, is that no one knows for certain which of these events will happen and which won't surface. All we do know is that some, or all, of this could happen.

Why? That's because of a vast array of computer electronics systems that are date and time sensitive, but to which date and time is unknown until the year arrives. If a computer's processor chip is programmed to read 01/01/00 as the first day of the Year 2000, it should work properly. On the other hand, if it interprets that date as the first day of the year 1900, the system could function properly or it could shut down.

There is no doubt that Y2K problems will confront us, at least at some level. For one, there are far too many embedded systems to make certain that each and every one will work in good order come the millennium. For another, there are millions upon millions of lines of computer programming code that need to be verified to make sure things continue to run.

Consider just one company and its situation. Canaccord Capital, based in Vancouver, British Columbia, has tripled the number of brokerage accounts it services through acquisition and merger. The firm is converting those accounts from other computer platforms to its own system, which is Y2K-compliant (meaning that it will handle the date appropriately). The conversion is actually being done to make it easier to manage a business whose customer base stretches from one end of Canada to the other. But the side benefit, said Drew McLennan, manager of computer services, is that Y2K problems should be eliminated.

That's good news for Canaccord, and for its customers. But if your bank or brokerage isn't up to date, how can you know your money will be safe? Yes, the United States provides deposit insurance for individuals of up to $100,000 in each account, but a company's accounts may lack that protection. Many banks are making great efforts to ensure that there are no breakdowns, but not every bank will be ready. Nor will every brokerage.

The exponential growth of computer technology in the past few decades has brought immeasurable benefits to individuals, organizations, and societies. At my desk in Los Angeles, using the technology of the Internet, I can listen to the BBC's World Service radio broadcasts without having a short-wave receiver. The BBC puts its broadcast on "the Net," as the Internet is known, and because I have an active connection and the proper software, I can hear the broadcast from London, some 5,000 miles away, as if I were right there. That's just one small example of what having a computer can do for one individual.

For organizations—both for profit and nonprofit—the computer revolution has made incredible things possible. The bulk of jobs being created in the United States and in many countries overseas are related in one way or another to technology. Fifty years ago, the city of San Jose, California, and the valley communities just north were sleepy little farming towns, by and large; today the

Silicon Valley is home to tens of thousands of high-tech workers in thousands of companies. Affluence abounds as luxury car dealers open larger and larger showcases for their wares. Young people barely out of college have stock worth enough money that they can retire before age thirty-five, if they want to.

In the nonprofit world, the arrival of computer technology has shaved manifold amounts of time off the work of serving people around the world. Here's just one example: The Salvation Army, a Christian church and relief agency headquartered in London, used to need a fortnight to send instructions to field offices in Africa and Asia. Now, using the Internet and a software package called Lotus Notes, the group can dispatch those instructions in seconds, and for a cost of pennies instead of the usual thirty dollars for each express package.

For societies, the arrival of computer technology has had an impact as well. In the United States, the economic boom created by computers has funded a variety of social service and educational projects, museums, and health initiatives. In other nations—India and the former Soviet Union to name two—the computer revolution has created jobs for many thousands. As Microsoft cofounder and chairman Bill Gates told a Moscow audience a couple of years back, there is no longer a need for skilled technology professionals to emigrate, leaving behind family and friends. Instead, the work they want to do can reach them via the Internet.

Thus, there's little denying the hold computerization has on society as part of our daily lives. Even if you have refused to let a PC into your home, the influence of computer technology touches everything from your television service (programmed and delivered via computer,

23

especially via cable and satellite systems) to your appliances (such as "smart" ranges, refrigerators, and, of course, the microwave), to medicine (got a pacemaker?), to money (just visit your ATM or use a credit card).

The potential for failure of these systems can range from the annoying—how will we record our favorite sitcom?—to the life threatening. If our favorite TV show isn't on tape, that may be disappointing, but it likely would not be catastrophic. If, on the other hand, a hospital's life-support system fails, the results could be far more severe.

This is the specter that hangs over us as the clock ticks down to the millennium. For some, such as Thomas L. Clark in Chicago, the time for action came early. A member of the Forrest Preserve Bible Church, Clark told me he is stocking up on food, has a hand mill for grinding grain into flour, and may decamp to the wilderness in advance of the first day of next year.

"Every day I study to see if there's anything sufficient being done, and I've found nothing to convince me that we won't have one massive problem," Clark, who labels himself an "informed fundamentalist," said. "This is going to rearrange my whole life."

In fact, it already has. Clark runs a business called Y2K Prepare, and from its Website of the same name, he sells food mills and offers tips on how to store food and water against the crisis he sees coming.[8]

This book is not an effort to gloss over the potential problems of the Y2K bug, nor is it an attempt to scare you out of your socks. Instead, I will examine the potential outcomes of mild, major, and severe "millennium bug" problems. The assessments you will read will come from leaders in science, business, industry, technology, and government, as well as from various branches of the Christian church. In almost every instance, you will see these claims backed up with an endnote indicating the source of the information. The goal here is to present fact, not fiction.

As a result, I believe you will find, in these pages, the most accurate information available at the time this book went to press, and you will have a guide to electronic links on the Internet with which you can remain updated. (A special section of the author's Website, www.kellner2000.com, offers links to the latest data.)

The Greatest Opportunity

Perhaps the greatest opportunity that the Year 2000 situation presents to Christians is that of not only being ministers to those less fortunate in their communities, but also to give a witness to the entire world by being helpful at a time which could be characterized by great selfishness. Our motivation is love, and our potential for witness is greater than any time since the first Pentecost.

In that spirit, consider the counsel given by the Assemblies of God, one of the largest denominations in America as well as one of the fastest growing in recent years. While arguing against food hoarding and the like, the church's General Council suggested another course:

> Instead the body of Christ should place its focus upon sharing our faith with those whose hearts are fearful about the future. In these hours when the world is filled with uncertainty, we have the message of hope from our Lord who has taught us to "Fear not." Rather than fearing the collapse of computers or society, the Scriptures call upon us to fear God's wrath. The good news is that God's wrath

needs never be experienced when we place our trust in Jesus as Savior and Lord.[9]

Whether or not the worst predictions about the Year 2000 come to pass, the advice above is not bad for believers to follow at any time. In the next chapter we'll see more of what could happen and how this started.

Endnotes

1. Dr. Jerry Falwell, telephone interview with author, 10 Nov. 1998.

2. Andres Rothovius, "In Search of New Year's Eve, A.D. 999," *Old Farmer's Almanac* (1999): 208.

3. Rupert Cornwell, "Nuclear Worries over Year 2000 Bug," *The Independent* newspaper, London, England, 12 Nov. 1998: 20.

4. Senator Robert Bennett, "U.S. Senate Committee on Commerce, Science, and Transportation holds hearing on potential impact of Y2K problems and what is being done to correct them," Washington Transcript Service, 28 April 1998.

5. Lisa M. Bowman, "Will Y2K Wreak Prison Havoc?" Ziff-David News Network, 11 Dec. 1998.

6. Mark A. Kellner, "Y2K—A Secular Apocalypse?" *Christianity Today*, 11 Jan. 1999.

7. Edward W. Kelley, Jr., Annual Economic Summit, Houston Baptist University, Washington Transcript Service, 29 Oct. 1998.

8. Quoted in Kellner.

9. Official statement, Assemblies of God, 14 Oct. 1998, quoted in Kellner.

Chapter 2

How Did We Get Here?

But you, Daniel, close up and seal the words of the scroll until the time of the end. Many will go here and there to increase knowledge.

Then I, Daniel, looked, and there before me stood two others, one on this bank of the river and one on the opposite bank. One of them said to the man clothed in linen, who was above the waters of the river, "How long will it be before these astonishing things are fulfilled?"

Daniel 12:4-6

These words from the Old Testament prophet, Daniel, are most often cited in connection with specific interpretations by teachers and preachers who are advancing this or that timetable for the fulfillment of such prophecies. But it may also be useful to ponder Daniel's words in the light of the Year 2000 situation. And instead of asking, "How long shall it be to the end of these wonders?" we might instead inquire, "Just *how* did we get here?"

Who Blinked When the Future Rushed Past?

This whole Y2K thing wasn't supposed to happen, at least not in the way it appears to be shaping up. Just look at the history of computers over the last fifty years or so.

There were not supposed to be that many computers around. When Thomas J. Watson, Sr., the former cash register salesman whose International Business Machines Corp. would dominate the computer industry for decades, cast an eye out over the market in 1943, he came up with this now breathtaking assessment: "I think there is a world market for maybe five computers."[1]

Fifty-six years later, I usually have more than five computers in my home. Granted, that's a high number, even for someone who writes daily about information technology. On the other hand, you may have at least one PC at home, and almost certainly confront one or more at your office or school. If your work is on an assembly line or in a service business, you will still encounter computers on the line or when entering a lunch order or when you visit the Automated Teller Machine at the bank, because that's a computer.

Of course, we can't be too hasty in judging Watson. He grew up in a mechanical age, before micro-circuitry, and those early computers would fill the entire square footage of a nice-sized house, not a small spot under the desk or . . . gasp . . . on one's lap. The cost of all those early vacuum tubes and wires and circuits (in 1943, the transistor was yet to arrive) was astronomical. The notion of the computer being widely popular back then would have been the stuff of fantasy and science fiction, not the thoughts of a hard-nosed businessman such as Mr. Watson.

Kenneth Olson was the MIT-educated engineer and equally hard-nosed founder of Digital Equipment Corp. whose *mini-computers* would give IBM's *mainframes* a run for their money—and customers. He was no less wrong when, in 1977, he suggested: "There is no reason for any individual to have a computer in the home."[2]

Perhaps unbeknownst to Olson, at about that time, two young men in Silicon Valley, Steve Wozniak and Steve Jobs, were creating the first Apple computer. Meanwhile, two other young men, Harvard dropout Bill Gates and his high school pal Paul Allen, were creating a programming language for the Altair, an early computer. Not long after, Gates settled upon a name for the new venture: Micro-soft (the hyphen would be dropped later).

But between Watson's cautious assessments, Olson's pessimism, the early ventures of "the two Steves" (as Wozniak and Jobs were called) and the early actions of the two Microsoft founders, there were several key developments which helped lead to today's looming crisis.

The seemingly remarkable speed with which this chain of events unfolded is, actually, decades long. Understanding some of the history of computing, as well as some of the specifics of how computers work and control many of the key aspects of our lives, will help us understand what happened and why.

A Brief History of Computers[3]

Starting in the seventeenth century, several European thinkers began to design and make various calculating devices. Counting numbers, and the things numbers represented, was important to a society which was fast developing trade routes with the East and this burgeoning country in the West called America.

Blaise Pascal is a name not unknown to Christians for his *Pensees,* or "Thoughts," a book of meditations based on his monastic experiences. (He wrote, "If God does not exist, one stands to lose nothing by believing in Him anyway, while if He does exist, one stands to lose everything by not believing.") But before his conversion in 1654, he was—and remained—a mathematician and scientist. Between 1641 and 1645 (historical references vary), he invented the "Pascaline," which is an early calculator. Though the device could not subtract, its success was the talk of Paris's intellectual community. (And besides having his *Pensees* survive to today, his name was also given to an early computer programming language, Pascal.)

Over the next 230 years, other inventors ranging from Gottfried Wilhelm von Leibniz of Leipzig, Germany, to Charles, the third Earl of Stanhope, to Charles Xavier Thomas de Colmar of France, each tinker with calculating machinery. De Colmar is the most successful, producing a kind of device that sells for more than 90 years. Along the way, a Hessian army officer, J. H. Mueller, conceives of a "difference engine," which tabulates the values of a polynomial, an advanced mathematical expression.

Charles Babbage, a British inventor, seizes upon this idea, and seeks to build a difference engine in the 1840s. Though not a total success, his research and plans spark a wide range of thinking about computations of numbers and data. Part of Babbage's designs included the use of cards with strategically punched holes for tabulating data. Such a concept was becoming a necessity: By the late 1800s, the long-anticipated blooming of global commerce was more than a notion; it was a fact.

Another fact was the growth in population of the United States, not long past its centennial celebration of the Declaration of Independence, and with many "huddled masses" having arrived in this country came a need for an accurate head count.

Article 1, Section 2 of the United States Constitution provided for an "enumeration" of the population "every ten years," and in 1880 the Bureau of the Census attracted the talents of Herman Hollerith, a son of German immigrants who was a skilled mathematician and a graduate of Columbia University. Hollerith came up with a punch-card scheme of his own, the story goes, not from Babbage's work, but from watching a ticket-taker on the bus. For the 1890 Census, Hollerith's punch card reader was all the rage, allowing officials to do far more in terms of analyzing and tabulating data than ever before.

According to the National Inventors Hall of Fame in Akron, Ohio, "Hollerith's system—including punch, tabulator, and sorter—allowed the official 1890 population count to be tallied in six months, and in another two years all the census data was completed and defined; the cost was $5 million below the forecasts and saved more than two years' time."[4]

Hollerith's tabulating system could be used to count more than just heads, of course. In 1896, he founded the Tabulating Machine Company, later to be known as the Computer Tabulating Recorder Company, into which a young man named Thomas J. Watson, Sr., mentioned earlier in this chapter, would later be recruited. CTR was renamed International Business Machines Corp., or IBM.

In 1935, IBM released the "IBM 601," a punch card machine with an arithmetic unit based on electrical relays. It could do multiplication in one second. Scientific and business users flocked to the machine, and some 1,500 were made.

Up to and during the Second World War, scientists in Britain, Germany, and the United States are at work on better and better calculating devices. Some of these are used to "break" the secret code language used by enemy forces (the British-born "Enigma" machine helped cripple Nazi efforts on several fronts by cracking coded messages). In the United States, such efforts are conducted under the Army's Ballistics Research Lab. The project is given the name ENIAC, which stood for "Electronic Numerator, Integrator, Analyzer, and Computer," and it attracts scientists such as John von Neumann, John W. Mauchly, and J. Presper Eckert. Although not ready for use during the war, ENIAC—revealed to the public in 1946—attracts the attention of many, including the business community.

Three years earlier, Harvard University scientist Howard H. Aiken had introduced the first large-scale calculator, which was refined into a larger model, the "Harvard Mark II," in 1947. One month after the machine was unveiled, a moth flew into the registers used to perform calculating functions. A technician removed the insect's remains, pasted them in a logbook, and noted it as the "first actual case of [a] bug being found."[5] One of the people who worked with Aiken on the Mark II, and later the Mark III, was Grace Murray Hopper (1906-1992), one of the few women of her day to earn a doctorate in mathematics (Yale, 1934). She was a military wife (her husband died in combat during the Second World War) and a member of the U.S. Naval Reserve.

Her mathematical skills were legendary; she was called "Amazing Grace," with no disrespect intended to the hymn of that title. Her motto was "Dare and Do," something she took from undergraduate studies to her doctoral thesis and shared with her students along the way. Her experiences in teaching "plain English" sentences to the earliest computers led her to help define the COBOL computer language, one of the first programming languages for mainframes. COBOL, which stands for "common business-oriented language," was launched in 1960. According to one estimate, there are perhaps 9.5 million COBOL applications running on systems today.[6]

Rear Admiral Hopper was fond of sharing a one-foot strand of wire, saying this represented "a nanosecond, since it was the maximum distance electricity could travel in wire in one-billionth of a second."[7] This would be contrasted with a thousand-foot coil of wire, which she said represented a microsecond. Her counsel to programmers was to not even waste a microsecond in writing programs.

While celebrated for her achievements—honors that included some thirty honorary doctorates and culminated with the 1997 commissioning of the USS Hopper, a U.S. Navy battleship—Grace Hopper may have, unwittingly, helped plant the seeds of the current crisis. When you "don't even waste a microsecond" in the writing of a computer program, unintended consequences can result.

Hold the Century, Please

In this case, the unintended consequence was the omission of the century from computer-recorded dates. Think back to Herman Hollerith and his tabulation cards, to Mauchly and Eckert and the ENIAC and then back to Grace Hopper and COBOL. In each instance, the pioneers didn't have a lot to work with.

The computer on which I am writing these words boasts a Central Processing Unit, or *CPU*, chip that contains 7.5 million transistors. Each transistor is the equivalent of an electronic switch, or bridge, allowing the processor to turn electrical impulses into data. That's a highly simplified explanation of some of what goes on in the CPU of today's computers. Add in the vast amounts of memory—both the hard disk and the "random access memory," or *RAM*—and you've got a system infinitely more powerful than those first machines.

But the computing pioneers I referred to didn't have those luxuries. They had very limited amounts of power and memory with which to work. Such constraints have dogged computing for decades. As a result, programmers and engineers followed Grace Hopper's dictum with almost slavish devotion: they didn't waste any energy on what would seem to be "useless" information.

January, after all, is the first month of the year. You could signify that with a "1," or "01" if you wished. Either of these indicators would take less computer space or energy to process than it would to recognize and translate the word "January" from English into a binary number the computer would understand. The same applies to years. Fifty years ago, "00" would have had one—and only one—meaning to most people, that of "1900," the first year of this century.

Thus, a date such as January 1, 1985, could be pared down substantially. It might be "01-01-85," or it might—in certain programs—omit even the dashes, ending up as "010185." Early "spreadsheets," computer programs which were designed to handle mathematical calculations the way a word processor handles words, converted various dates—"25-March-89," for example—into a series of numbers which only the spreadsheet would recognize. (The screen would display the proper date, but the code would stand "behind" the date when it came to formulas and calculations.)

This economy, which began with ENIAC and evolved down to today's systems, seemed harmless enough. After all, who thought the computers of 1955 would still be running businesses in 1995? By the latter date, other systems would predominate and these would be better, faster, stronger. Indeed, back in 1965, Gordon Moore, a pioneer in semiconductor design who would later co-found Intel Corp., said each new computer CPU chip contained roughly twice as much capacity as its predecessor, and each was released within eighteen to twenty-four months of the previous chip. "Moore's Law," as it came to be known, has been an accurate predictor of the computer age's growth.[8]

Even with more capacity on computer processors—and concurrent upgrades in the amount of hard disk storage and RAM would be made available to users—developers were always adding other features to computers. Few were concerned about the way in which dates were processed. From the mere number crunching of the earliest computers, we moved on to the *data base,* a file of whatever was of interest: names and addresses of customers, an inventory, tax records, what-have-you. These advances and others yet to come would both increase the power of computing, and our dependence upon that power.

Birth of a Notion--the Personal Computer

By the mid-1970s, a variety of advances in electronics and engineering would combine to create a revolutionary idea: a computer that could fit on a desktop and be used by one person at a time. This "personal" computer was first the domain of hobbyists, users of the Altair system described earlier in the chapter. By 1980, Apple Computer's Apple II system was being used by cutting-edge businesses to manipulate information in ways previously unavailable to smaller firms. At about the same time, many companies were betting on something called the S-100 system bus—a way of building small computers—and an operating system called CP/M, or "Control Program for Microcomputers."

Then, in 1981 the floodgates burst open. IBM Corp. premiered a device it dubbed the IBM Personal Computer, or IBM PC. The size and market power of IBM would help push this device into companies of various sizes and shapes, at least on a trial basis.

Something, however, would come along to help propel the IBM PC from an also-ran into the ranks of a market leader. It was the open nature of the IBM system that prompted this. Instead of keeping everything about the computer *proprietary* (i.e., exclusive) to IBM, the company allowed outside firms to develop add-in products and peripheral devices for the new system. The operating software for the PC could be either CP/M or a new one, called MS-DOS, for MicroSoft Disk Operating System. Applications developers could create software for the operating system, and not the specific computer, which was another revolutionary change.

A man named Mitch Kapor, along with some other programmers, developed one of those applications. It was called 1-2-3, and it was a spreadsheet as easy to use as, well, counting one, two, and three. The software was extremely powerful, fast, and could render a pie chart or bar graph of the data. It had a tutorial showing you how to use the software. Sales took off like a rocket, boosting sales of the only computer on which it would run, the IBM PC.

All of these factors combined to propel computing into the national consciousness. Today, almost every desk in an office will have a PC on it; and millions of executives and managers and marketers carry notebook computers on their travels.

Along the way, computer chips have been used to power other devices. Following Moore's Law, as new PC chips came on the scene, the older ones, now less expensive (and less capable) were shunted to other tasks. They became part of so-called "embedded systems," in which a computer chip and some hard-wired software control a given device. Instead of having a factory, a sewer system, or an assembly line controlled by supervisors and workers who used their own brainpower, this was transferred to the "intelligence" of the computer chip. Utopia, we were told, lay just around the corner as people were freed from much of the drudgery such mundane tasks entailed.

The good—and bad—news that follows from this is that while computers of every stripe were permeating just about every aspect of society, no one, and no group, was checking to see the effects of this. No one was checking to see what kinds of computers were being installed, and where, and to what end. The result would be the potential for a digital equivalent of a "death by a thousand cuts," where a slice here and a stab there, nonlethal in and of themselves, could cumulatively lead to massive problems.

As older technology was being buried in less-critical systems, it also found its way into critical systems. You didn't *need* the latest CPU just to open and close valves at the water treatment plant; any one that would respond to a set of commands is fine. If your mainframe computer ran out of capacity to handle a growing number of bank accounts, don't worry. Just get a later system, *but use the same software and data files*, only on a larger scale.

Without a centralized control—something that would be anathema in a free society such as the U.S., and ultimately unmanageable in the Communist world—there was no way to monitor the situation and see a burgeoning problem until it was too late.

Even though the U.S. federal government should have been able to foresee a problem, it was nearly thirty years behind in adopting a solution. From 1968 to 1996, the National Institute of Standards and Technology, formerly known as the National Bureau of Standards, had a "Federal Information Processing Standard," or "FIPS," which decreed a six-digit date format, such as 010199 (forget the dashes and slashes). Only three years ago did the Institute wise up to the idea of an eight-digit date format (01011999).[9]

In February 1984, Paul Gillin was a reporter for *Computerworld,* the industry's first computer weekly and its most successful. He got a call from William Schoen, a programmer in Detroit. Schoen had the notion that a lot of computers would stop working on New Year's Day, 2000. An article appeared in the weekly publication, and while it was one of many accomplishments that helped make Gillin the editor-in-chief of the magazine, it did little for Schoen. The programmer was trying to sell a "Year 2000" remediation kit—a software solution that would fix the date problem. He sold a total of two before finding other work.

Indeed, as computer consultant Dave Schaller wrote

in a letter to the editor in *Computerworld,* in the early and mid 1980s, the Year 2000 issue "wasn't a problem at the time, and there wasn't a programmer in his right mind who would have suggested to management that changes be made to existing standards. . . . The more pressing issues were running a day-to-day business, implementing enhancements and keeping costs down."[10]

Keeping costs down. Those three words might well be the epitaph on the Y2K headstone. It's been estimated that had the work been done earlier, not only could severe problems have been avoided, but the cost of fixing all this would have been far less. Now, not only is it costing businesses trillions of dollars[11] to keep up with the Y2K situation (the insurance trade magazine *BestWeek* estimates that the top sixty insurance companies alone will spend more than $6.58 *billion* on Y2K fixes[12]), but also the impact of a world gone haywire could be even greater.

The Beginnings of a Response

Few may have been willing to listen to Bill Schoen in 1984—would that they had been!—but business and industry is now very willing to hear what the experts are saying. And a response is beginning to take shape.

For the tens of millions of personal computers that are out there, companies including Network Associates, Symantec Corp., and a host of smaller firms have released products designed to make PCs compliant with Y2K standards. We'll learn more about these solutions in a later chapter. For larger systems—mainframe computers which store utility records and other critical data—remediation efforts are starting to roll out.

According to a report in *The New York Times,* the

perception of the Y2K issue has changed dramatically: "It's the biggest business problem in human history," one expert told the paper.[13]

Beginning a few years ago, some companies began working diligently to solve their Y2K issues. This conduct escalated in 1997 and 1998; the year of 1999 is expected to see such efforts reach a fever pitch.

Middle-aged—and I use that term advisedly—programmers whose COBOL skills relegated them to a Jurassic Era of data processing are suddenly in demand. The Bank of America is paying top dollar for such programmers and promising those who stay a bonus of up to $75,000—half payable after May 2000[14]. Others are being lured back to work with promises of lavish compensation and royal treatment on the road.

Bruce Fassett, a "retired" Motorola Corp. COBOL programmer had one week's respite after accepting a corporate buyout from that firm's Phoenix, Arizona operations. Within seven days, he was snapped up by giant computer services firm Electronic Data Systems, Inc., of Dallas, given a hefty increase on his former $60,000-per-year salary, and a raft of benefits: EDS provided "a $4\frac{1}{2}$ day workweek and agreed to let him live anywhere in the United States near a major airport," according to a *Los Angeles Times* report. When Fassett's work takes him away from home, EDS provides "free lawn care, pet care, covered airport parking, spousal flights and dry cleaning."[15]

Fassett's experience is not unique. Remember the bit about an estimated 9.5 *million* COBOL systems running in business today? Those systems need fixing, and to do that, you've got to find thousands and thousands of Bruce Fassetts.

That work is continuing at a breakneck pace, with the

gamble being that enough will be fixed so as to cause only mild disruption. The Gartner Group research firm, one of the most respected in information technology circles, is betting on disruptions lasting no more than a week in most cases. Others are anticipating far more difficult circumstances. In the next chapter, we'll begin to examine what could happen if things begin to breakdown.

Endnotes

1. Quoted in *The Experts Speak* by Victor Navasky (n.c.: Villard Books, 1998), as cited in "Many Predictions from the Past Missed Mark Badly," *Minneapolis Star Tribune*, 1 Dec. 1995: 02D.

2. Quoted in "Some Faulty Foresight," Gannett News Service, 3 March 1997: S12.

3. In this chapter, I am indebted to Mark Brader, who created "A Chronology of Digital Computing Machines (to 1952)," which is published on the Internet at the "alt.folklore.computers List of Frequently Asked Questions." Brader's research, plus my own online searching, forms the basis for the initial part of this section.

4. "1995 National Inventors Hall of Fame Black Book," online (http://www.invent.org/book/book-text/57.html).

5. Noted in "A Chronology of Digital Computing Machines (to 1952)," online (www.best.com/wilson/faq/chrono.html).

6. C. F. Capers Jones, quoted in "The Cutting Edge: Bug Re-Boots COBOL Experts' Fading Careers," by Ashley Dunn, *Los Angeles Times*, 21 Sept. 1998: C1.

7. Cited in "Grace Murray Hopper," Website maintained by Yale University (www.cs.yale.edu/HTML/YALE/CS/HyPlans/tap/Files/hopper-story.html).

8. "What Is Moore's Law," Intel Corp. Website (www.intel.com/intel/museum/25anniv/Hof/moore.htm).

9. Cited in Tenner, Edward, "Chronologically Incorrect (year 2000 computer date transition problem)," *The Wilson Quarterly* 22 (22 Sept. 1998): 27.

10. Dave Schaller in "Letters," *Computerworld,* 28 Sept. 1998: 32.

11. Cited in "Year 2000 Risk Assessment and Planning for Individuals," Gartner Group, Stamford, CT, 28 Oct. 1998, online (gartner4.gartnerweb.com/public/static/home/00073955.html#0001).

12. Cited in "Insurers Y2K Costs Could Top $6.58 Billion," *Best-Week,* 14 Dec. 1998, online (www.bestweek.com/issue-pc/1998/sr121698.html).

13. Capers Jones, quoted in "Computers and Year 2000: A Race for Security (and Against Time)," by Barnaby J. Feder and Andrew Pollack, *The New York Times,* 27 Dec. 1998: 1.

14. Cited in Feder and Pollack.

15. Cited in Dunn.

Chapter 3

What May Happen

There will be great distress in the land and wrath against this people. . . . There will be signs in the sun, moon and stars. On the earth, nations will be in anguish and perplexity at the roaring and tossing of the sea. Men will faint from terror, apprehensive of what is coming on the world, for the heavenly bodies will be shaken.

Luke 21:23, 25-26

What Luke, the physician and apostle, writes here are the words of Jesus in relation to the last days, that time just before Christ returns to earth and the kingdom of God is established for all time. Some Christians, seeing the potential problems created by the Y2K computer bug, believe that this may be the final catastrophe that will usher in the end of the world. Some non-Christians, too, feel that we are facing an apocalypse. Where is the truth here?

It's not for me to say in this book (or anywhere else, for that matter) that the dawn of the next millennium will mark the return of Jesus Christ, the end of this system, and the inauguration of the heavenly kingdom. That could happen—and it could not happen. As noted earlier in chapter one, Jesus himself was explicit about this: "But of that day and hour knoweth no man, no, not the angels of heaven, but my Father only," he said in Matthew 24:36 (KJV). I can't tell you when Jesus will return, and, frankly, neither can anyone else.

That said, it's worth remembering Jesus' description of what the end times would be like, if only to use as a yardstick against which we can measure what happens in the Year 2000. If the worst, humanly, does happen, then society could indeed be in for a time of "great distress" that has had no equal until this point. But there are lots of other possibilities.

Is This the Beginning of Sorrows?

For some people, this disaster scenario is the one that Y2K conjures up: a world without banks, electricity, or water. No safe perishable food in your grocery store, and no gas for your car. Mass panic in your community, with perhaps the military on each corner securing stores against looters.

People in the San Fernando Valley of Los Angeles don't have to imagine these things—they lived them just five years ago. They occurred in the first hours and days after the January 17, 1994, Northridge earthquake, which struck at 4:31 A.M. with devastating force. Driving through the streets, I saw National Guardsmen patrolling outside a Sears store. I saw spoiled food at supermarkets. I went to the swimming pool in my apartment complex to fill a bucket so I could flush the toilet in my home. One bank in our neighborhood was truly "open for business"—all the windows in its glass façade had shattered, and only a police guard kept people from rushing in.

Similar scenes, of course, followed flooding in the Midwest in 1993, Hurricane Andrew in Florida a year earlier, and other disasters in other parts of the world. Even a moderately severe winter storm—a seemingly normal occurrence in many parts of the country—can wreak havoc, as storms have already done in 1999. Stores were flooded in advance of these storms with people seeking milk and other perishables; replacement supplies were at times difficult to come by.

Should the Y2K bug hit with full force—and no one knows for certain how devastating the hit is going to be, or how mild—we could see similar societal disruptions on a nationwide scale. In this chapter, we'll get an overview of what might go wrong and where.

Hurry Midnight?

Just when does the clock change to January 1, 2000?

The stroke of midnight is the somewhat arbitrary point at which we determine the end of one day and the beginning of the next. But when is midnight, exactly? Is it at 12:00 A.M. in the Pacific Time zone, where I'm sitting, or at the same hour in the Central Time zone, where my editor resides? Perhaps it's at midnight in New York City, where my parents make their home.

At one point in history, the United States had as many as 300 local time zones. Led by the railroad industry, on November 18, 1883, the United States adopted as the official time standard "Greenwich Mean Time," established in the 1840s as the correct time on the prime meridian, which runs through Greenwich, England. The

U.S. mainland was divided into four time zones. Less than a year later, on November 1, 1884, the International Meridian Conference was held in Washington and from that point, an International Date Line was drawn up and twenty-four worldwide time zones created.

What all that means, effectively, is that the New Year of 2000 will officially dawn when the clock strikes midnight in Greenwich, England, on December 31, 1999, which will be 7:00 P.M. in New York, and 4:00 P.M. that afternoon in Los Angeles. That hour in Greenwich, England—not our local midnights—could be the time when our troubles begin.

Tests Reveal Potential Problems

Whenever midnight hits, things could grind to a halt if the worst scenarios prevail. As mentioned in earlier chapters, if a computer misreads "010100" as January 1, 1900, there could be all sorts of consequences. Here are some examples, taken from early tests:

- BAA Plc, a British-based operator of airports, ran a test of systems at the airport in Brussels, Belgium, simulating a Year 2000 date. The results? Security card readers couldn't read the access cards that admit authorized employees to certain areas of the airport. A baggage sorting system sent all the luggage down the "unsorted" chute. And the security system couldn't recognize a fire alarm signal.[1]
- A chemical mixing system at Amway Corp. in Ada, Mich., rejected some chemicals when a "bad" date showed up under Y2K testing.[2]
- Some 2,013 customers of Bank One, Texas, a unit of Ohio-based Bank One Corp., were surprised to

receive overdraft notices claiming checks had bounced on their accounts. The notices were bogus, generated during a dry run of a Y2K test, and were mailed out due to "human error," the bank said. Customer anger, however, was real.[3]

- The Internal Revenue Service sent out delinquency notices to taxpayers, again in error during Y2K testing. (If you think an overdrawn check notice is bad news, just try getting an erroneous $300 million bill from the tax collector!)[4]

- An audit of the Houston, Texas, Public Works and Engineering Department revealed potential Y2K glitches that would disable the city's water billing system, responsible for $500 million a year in revenues. Auditors Deloitte & Touche "took the unusual step recently of halting their work in mid-audit to raise the alarm about the water customer information system," according to a *Houston Chronicle* report.[5]

These examples show what might happen in several circumstances. There are many more test results coming to light every day, some revealing good news and others potentially critical problems.

When reading such scenarios, it's tempting to dismiss these as wild-eyed speculation, or the rants of a Bible-thumping dispensationalist. But listen, for a moment, to some people who are neither uninformed nor religious zealots.

FCC Chairman William Kennard, being questioned by the U.S. Senate, concluded, "[I am] concerned that the year 2000 problem has the potential of disrupting communications services worldwide. . . . Every sector of the communications industry—broadcast, cable, radio, satellite, and wireline and wireless telephony—could be affected."[6]

Michehl R. Gent, president of the North American Electric Reliability Council, told a Senate subcommittee on June 12, 1998, that the nation's electrical supply is interconnected within each of four power-grid regions: the Eastern Interconnection, which covers the eastern two-thirds of North America, including Canada; the Western Interconnection, covering much of the western U.S. and Canada, as well as Baja California in Mexico; the "ERCOT" region, which covers most of Texas; and Quebec, a Canadian province. Gent told lawmakers: "Each of these four Interconnections is a highly connected network. . . . A major disturbance within one part of an Interconnection has the potential to cascade through the entire Interconnection."

While Gent believes that the Year 2000 won't trigger massive power outages, he made room for one potential exception: "Y2K poses the threat that common mode failures, such as all generator protection relays of a particular model failing simultaneously, or the coincident loss of multiple facilities could result in stressing the electric system to the point of a cascading outage over a large area," he said, although he emphasized such a possibility was "extremely low, but conceivable."[7]

If these two experts are to be believed, there's a slight chance that significant parts of North America could be without telephone service and electrical power come January 1, 2000. What about matters of public safety and municipal systems? According to Bruce Romer, Chief Administrative Officer for Montgomery County, Maryland, a suburb of Washington, D.C., there's a potential for trouble on this front if the power grid fails in a major way.

If not fixed, this problem threatens public safety, emergency response, health and human services, finance, taxation, permitting, and even the operation of traffic management systems. In combination, problems in these areas could lead to challenges for public safety organizations, stoppage of critical services, loss of revenue, and enormous potential litigation costs," Romer told the Senate Y2K Subcommittee in October 1998.[8]

Not Just North America

With the clock ticking away towards the next millennium, it's useful perhaps to note that these problems are not limited to North America. According to Graeme Inchley, head of Australia's Year 2000 initiatives, that country won't be fully ready for the Year 2000 and can only hope to fix major systems, devising "workarounds" for others.[9] In Britain, Don Cruickshank, who heads the government's "Action 2000" committee, is seeking contingency plans for national failures under the Y2K bug.[10]

On December 11, 1998, United Nations Secretary-General Kofi Annan, addressing a special Year 2000 conference, said a Y2K disruption "will be felt through the global interdependencies of trade, manufacturing, transport, energy generation and distribution, telecommunications and defense technology." Representatives from more than 130 countries gathered to consider what might happen and how to resolve it, while admitting that precious little time remains for a solution.[11] That U.N. meeting grew out of a General Assembly resolution voicing concern over the potential impact of the Y2K situation.

In a press statement, the U.N. said,

> The impact on developing countries is even more of an unknown quantity. Although computer systems are much less pervasive in developing countries than in those with advanced technologies, a larger share of their systems likely rely on older software that has not been updated to offset the effect. Most developing country governments and businesses have less money and fewer local experts available to them than is the case in industrialized countries, and a number of governments of developing countries are preoccupied by natural catastrophes or civil conflicts.
>
> In all countries, air traffic control, telecommunications, financial services and government services are at particular risk. . . . Moreover, economists worry that business setbacks may lead to destabilization of international financial markets, which have not yet recovered fully from the 1997-1998 [world economic] crisis.[12]

According to Pakistan's U.N. ambassador, Ahmad Kamal, "The consequences of unpreparedness in any one country can rapidly spill over to other parts of the world."[13]

International bankers and financiers recognize the potential for problems involving the Year 2000. Addressing the House Committee on Banking and Finance in June 1998, Federal Reserve Bank of New York first vice president Ernest T. Patrikis was blunt in his assessment:

> Nearly all financial organizations worldwide are potentially at risk. Even those whose own operations

remain strictly paper-based are likely to be dependent on power, water, and telecommunications utilities which [sic] must themselves address possible Y2K problems. Also, many non-financial customers have dependencies on technology.[14]

Think Globally, Worry Locally

Senator Robert Bennett, a Republican from Utah, is the son of a United States Senator and a successful businessman who headed what is now Franklin Covey, Inc., before going to Washington. He chairs the Senate's subcommittee on Y2K and gave a chilling assessment to the National Press Club on July 15, 1998, of what might happen. High on his list was the matter of what could develop with computer chips that are embedded in various systems.

> If all of a sudden the pipeline that is bringing natural gas to the generating plant that is creating the electricity that's lighting these lights shuts down because an imbedded chip in one of the valves fails, it isn't just a valve in a pipeline that has failed, the whole power grid is now at risk. And if enough of them fail in enough key places, you don't have any power. Or, if enough of them fail in enough water purification plants, you don't have any water. Or, if enough of them fail in enough medical devices in an ICU in a major hospital, some people will die.

However, Senator Bennett added that the U.S., Canada, Britain, Australia, and Singapore are among nations working most diligently on the Y2K problem and therefore least likely to have major problems. "Japan, Germany, France, and many of our other allies" are not in the "top tier" of nations working on this. Other observers indicate that China and Russia (as well as other member states of the now-defunct Soviet Union) are also tardy in their Y2K remediation.[15]

Under questioning from Douglas Harbrecht, Washington News Editor of *Business Week* magazine and, at the time, president of the National Press Club, Bennett gave further forecasts about what will happen domestically during the initial phases of the Year 2000:[16]

- The national power grid will work, mostly. "There will be brownouts and some blackouts," he said. But "there's a 40 percent chance" that it will fail overall.
- While the financial system is expected to remain intact, there may be some problems: "I think you will still be able to trade stocks on the New York Stock Exchange. I wouldn't want to trade stocks on the Nikkei in Tokyo, but I think the security system will probably work. I think the banking system will work. I think there are individual banks that will probably go bankrupt."
- "Water will be available in most municipalities," Bennett said, "but I am convinced there are some where the water system will break down. And there could be serious, serious difficulty in those communities."
- On health care, the senator's concerns are both financial and technical: "There are health care entities that may very well go bankrupt because they cannot get reimbursement from Medicare and Medicaid. There are medical machines that will fail

in ICU units. There are hospitals that are far enough away from other hospitals that they have no back-up, and if they have a failure in some of their machines or in some of their supplies, there will be people who will be affected."

■ He added that he was worried about the functioning of counties: "What's going to happen to the social fabric in this country if a county in a large, populous area cannot deliver welfare checks?"

The "bottom line" from the one man in Congress who may have studied the issue more than any other? Think about some preparations: "I'm not yet ready to start storing food in the basement and digging up the back yard to put in a propane tank, but it might not be a bad idea to have a little extra food and water around in case the supermarket can't get its stocks for seventy-two hours or a week or two because of breakdowns in the transportation system."

Such a statement must be viewed, however, from two perspectives. One, as a public official, Senator Bennett likely feels responsible for helping maintain an attitude of calm in the public sector. In his speech, he eschewed the "Chicken Little" attitude that would say "the sky is falling." However, as you can see, his remarks were punctuated with some serious concerns about the worst possible outcomes.

Also, he made these remarks on July 15, 1998, with some seventy-three weeks to go before the Year 2000 hit. As I write these words, far less time remains—and less will be available when you read them. If hospitals, utilities, and financial institutions haven't made sufficient progress by the second quarter of 1999, it's quite possible in my view that Bennett may have a greater sense of urgency in his remarks.

Indeed, the potential for greater disruptions than those forecast by Bennett and others is what is fueling the great speculation we are seeing about the Year 2000. And others point out that panic, itself, could fuel disaster even if virtually every major system is prepared for the New Year. And much progress has been made.

But others in government seem to agree with Bennett. One of his Senate colleagues, Daniel Patrick Moynihan, senior Senator from New York and aide to Presidents Kennedy, Johnson, and Nixon, former ambassador to India and to the United Nations, is one man whose words aren't taken lightly. In October 1998, Moynihan had this to say about the potential woes a Y2K meltdown could cause. "Historically, the *fin de siècle* has caused quite a stir," Moynihan said, referring to the end of a time cycle that will be marked by the millennium:

> Until now, however, there has been little factual basis on which doomsayers and apocalyptic fear mongers could spread their gospel. After studying the potential impact of Y2K on the telecommunications industry, health care, economy, and other vital sectors of our lives, I would like to warn that we have cause for fear. For the failure to address the millennium bug could be catastrophic.[17]

The answer for most of us is to watch and wait—and, as people of faith, to pray. It's also useful to ponder what could happen in specific industries, and in the next chapter, we'll look at your money and what might be necessary to protect it.

Endnotes

1. Cited in "Airports Try to Head Off Millennium Bug Specter," by Suzanne Perry, Reuters News Service, 21 Dec. 1998.

2. Cited in "Y2K: So Many Bugs . . . So Little Time," by Peter de Jaeger, *Scientific American,* Jan. 1999; also in "Early Year 2000 Glitches Provide Sneak Preview," by Thomas Hoffman and Julia King, *Computerworld,* 28 Aug. 1998.

3. Dan Piller, "Bank One Texas Stung by the Y2K Bug during Systems Test," online, *Fort-Worth Star-Telegram,* 15 Dec. 1998.

4. Reuters News Service wire report, "IRS will be Year 2000 ready," 23 Oct. 1998.

5 . Julie Mason, "Audit raises red flag at Y2K glitch," *Houston Chronicle,* 7 Dec. 1998.

6. Cited in statement of Sgt. John S. Powell, Univ. of Calif. Police Dept., to Senate Special Committee on the Year 2000 Technology Problem, 2 Oct. 1998.

7. Prepared Testimony of Michehl R. Gent, before the U.S. Senate Special Committee on the Year 2000 Technology Problem, 12 June 1998.

8. Testimony of Bruce Romer on "Emergency Planning for the Year 2000: Preparation or Panic?" to Senate Special Committee on the Year 2000 Technology Problem, 2 Oct. 1998.

9. Quoted in "Australian Government Will Not Correct Everything, Says Y2K Expert," *Australian Financial Review,* 3 March 1998.

10. Quoted in "Britain's Y2K Official Seeks National Contingency Plans," *Computer Weekly,* 11 March 1998.

11. Quoted in "Global Y2K Conference at U.N.," United Press International dispatch, 11 Dec. 1998.

12. "Global Y2K Conference at U.N."

13. United Nations news release, 10 Dec. 1998.

14. Ernest T. Patrikis, testimony, "Year 2000 Challenge To International Banking System," U.S. House of Representatives, 23 June 1998.

15. Senator Bob Bennett, "Paul Revere Not Chicken Little: Who's Sounding the Call for the Year 2000?" transcript of remarks at National Press Club as found on Senate Y2K Subcommittee Website.

16. Ibid.

17. Senator Daniel Patrick Moynihan, Statement, "Small Business to Global Corporations: Will They Survive Year 2000?" Senate Subcommittee hearing, 7 Oct. 1998.

Chapter 4

The Day Your Money Dies?

Keep your lives free from the love of money and be content with what you have, because God has said, "Never will I leave you; never will I forsake you."

Hebrews 13:5 (quoting Deut. 31:6)

Go to the theatre district in New York City, and you may see a revival of one of the great musical plays of the latter part of the twentieth century. *Cabaret* is a rather frank and somewhat chilling look at the seamy side of life in Berlin, Germany, just before the start of World War II.

In a role brilliantly originated by Joel Grey, the emcee of the Kit Kat Klub night spot sings a refrain believed by many people of that era, the late 1920s and early 1930s: "Money makes the world go around . . . that clinking, clanking sound" makes the world go round!

Let's face it—even if our faith is rock-solid, without a shadow of turning, there may be the odd moment or two when we have some concern about how much money we have or what it's doing. For some, it's more comforting to know we have $40 or $50 in our wallets—even if our bank balance is low—than it might be to have $10,000 on deposit but no cash on hand.

One motivational speaker I have heard—a very good man of principle and integrity named Jim Rohn—once told an audience that they should have an extra $100 bill and carry it, folded, in their wallet or purse. "It'll make you feel more secure," he said. You may or may not agree with this (and I, for one, don't usually carry an extra "C note" around), but the sentiment Rohn expresses is one I can understand.

It may be one you understand, too. Going out with some cash—and certainly a credit card or two—is a part of American life these days for millions upon millions of us. Not long ago, after making a deposit at my bank, I saw the woman in line behind me walk up to a teller, present a credit card, and ask for a $1,500 cash advance as calmly as you or I might ask for a cup of coffee at a McDonald's counter. Watching this underscored, to me at least, the value some people can place on having quick cash available.

What is true of individuals is often true for businesses—and even for nonprofit organizations. The company that has access to a ready supply of capital can often outmaneuver the company with less money on hand. The ministry that can pay for a desirable piece of real estate, or bid for the employ of a top-drawer fund raiser, or procure air time on the "better" broadcast outlet in a given market will sometimes see its work flourish while other congregations languish.

None of this should be surprising to most readers, nor should it seem like a particular revelation—the simple truths of life are often like that. It could be argued, I believe, that Jesus recognized the power of money—and the usefulness of having some—when he caused the miraculous appearance of a coin in the mouth of a fish, just the amount needed to pay a tax (see Matthew 17:24-27). And while Paul, that wise rabbi from Tarsus, cautioned against believers cultivating a "love of money," he also enjoined other followers of Jesus to work and earn a living if they wanted to eat (see 2 Thessalonians 3:10).

Finally, I believe most of us can agree that money is a useful medium of exchange. The person who rents a home to us appreciates our gratitude, but she wants to see a check on the first of the month. I might barter one of my skills for someone else's talent, but it's less likely that I'll walk into Sears, write a short article for the salesperson, and leave with a new stove. If money doesn't exactly "make the world go 'round," for most of modern society, it surely helps grease the wheels.

Thus, the potential impact of the Year 2000 on finances is of great interest to millions of people. Indeed, the potential for financial collapse has motivated the actions of many observers and individuals. Layman Thomas Clark and evangelist Jerry Falwell—both of whom were quoted in chapter 1—each told me they fear the worst if the economic system can't function and if government payments do not reach the intended recipients. While United States Senator Robert Bennett is confident about this nation's financial system overall, remember that it was his membership in the Senate Banking Committee that brought him to the Year 2000 issue. And with the Federal Reserve Bank planning to print and distribute to banks between $25 billion and $50 billion in extra currency—enough to put as much as $500 in the hands of every man, woman, and child—the notion that a Millennium Bug could strike at the heart of our finances isn't mere speculation, if you'll allow that word to be used here.

A Potential Plethora of Problems?

January 1, 2000, is a Saturday. For many of us, it's a day on which our banks will either be closed or have limited hours. The next day is a Sunday, when *most* banks are closed. Therefore, that first weekend in the year 2000 most people may try to do their banking electronically. However, if utilities are affected there could be difficulties:

- If electrical power is out, the ATM at your corner store won't work. (Then again, your corner store wouldn't be open.)
- ATMs send the data of a transaction back and forth chiefly via telephone data lines. Any disruption in telephone service, caused by a malfunction in electrical service or a telephone switching system computer malfunction, could put the kybosh on a quick withdrawal of funds.
- Similarly, communication breakdowns could prevent you from using an ATM card, charge card, or debit card at the supermarket, gas station, or department store. This could also cut stores off from check verification services, making it less likely that your personal check would be accepted in stores where you are not well known.

Put any of these factors into the mix and that long weekend could stretch into a longer period of inconvenience. People unable to withdraw money from banks, and merchants unwilling to accept checks they may not be able to deposit and cash, would be in a stalemate to say the least. Bartering may make a comeback!

As should be obvious, we are an interconnected society. It's not enough for me to have money in the bank. The money has to be verifiable for a prudent merchant to honor my draft. That's why (and how) check verification services such as TeleCheck International, Inc., of Houston exist. That firm, by the way, serves 200,000 retail and financial institutions and other clients in the U.S., Canada, Australia, New Zealand, and Puerto Rico. In 1997, the firm processed some $98.3 billion in check authorizations, which represent over 1.9 billion checks. Using sophisticated computer and communications equipment, the firm can, in one-quarter of a second, perform a sophisticated computer scan to make sure that a check's issuer is a valid individual who isn't known for writing bad checks.[1]

TeleCheck began working on Year 2000 issues in 1993, and in August of 1998 sent a letter to customers stating that the firm's computer programs were updated for the Y2K issue. "Subscribers should be able to continue to use TeleCheck applications without any interruption of service through the Year 2000," Senior Vice President Hodges Marshall wrote.[2]

While that news is certainly encouraging, there is one potential catch, at least from my perspective. TeleCheck relies on information from subscribing financial institutions, and there, things could break down.

According to Ellen Seidman, director of the U.S. Treasury's Office of Thrift Supervision (OTS), as of March 1998, some 15 percent of banks regulated by her office were not sufficiently prepared for Y2K issues—they lacked "action plans" and had not made contact with vendors to determine whether their systems would be ready for the Year 2000.[3]

By September of 1998, Seidman told the House Banking Committee that things had gotten better but that one of the eight regional providers of ATM network services was "unsatisfactory" in its Y2K readiness (that firm was expected to liquidate its business by the end of 1998) and another "needed improvement" because it had not adequately checked its network services vendors.

As a result of this and other supervisory efforts, even though the OTS expects most savings banks to be ready for Y2K, Seidman told Representative Jim Leach, chairman of the House committee, "We expect that, no matter how well we are prepared, there will be glitches and problems." This is an encouraging picture unless the glitches are at your local bank.

The outlook for commercial banks and credit unions is—at this writing—somewhat unclear. On December 7, 1998, credit union regulators and officials met in Washington, D.C., to consider ways to raise the amount of money held in the "Central Liquidity Fund" which is one of the key underpinnings of credit union financial reliability. While executives of the credit union industry believe a run by depositors on credit unions isn't likely, media pressure could change that scenario.

"Press coverage could endanger the whole thing—if it's enough to put fear into credit union members. Right now that's not the case," said Bob Loftus, director of public and congressional affairs for the National Credit Union Association.[4]

Commercial banks, which fall under the aegis of the Federal Deposit Insurance Corp. and the Comptroller of the Currency, may be in better stead. NationsBank, the large southeastern U.S. bank group that recently merged with BankAmerica Corp., gave this December 1998 assessment of Y2K readiness: "Our Y2K project is well underway and our plan is to have renovation largely completed for mission-critical applications by the end of 1998. This will allow for broad testing and clean-up well before the year 2000."[5] However, the bank warns that such a proclamation is valid only on the date it has been made: "Due to the evolving nature of the year 2000 challenge, information may change."[6]

The Bank of America, which NationsBank acquired in the merger with its parent, said it planned to be Year 2000 ready by December 31, 1998. But, the Bank of America, adds, "we are also preparing contingency plans, which will be implemented, if required, to minimize interruptions to bank operations."[7]

You get the idea: While banks are planning for the best outcome, the prudent ones expect to be ready for the worst. At a minimum, a prudent individual would want to take steps to secure their financial situation well in advance of January 1, 2000.

What should you do? While it's always a wise tactic to discuss your needs with your accountant, lawyer, or other professional, I can suggest some basic ideas:[8]

1. *Have some ready cash.* More than one expert and/or advocate in the field has said that keeping some extra cash on hand is a good idea—anywhere from two week's worth to a month's worth of cash. Few people believe disruptions would last significantly beyond a month, so having vast cash reserves should be unnecessary. If storing such items at home, consider a good safe or other storage system. (If, on the other hand, you see more ominous signs as the deadline day approaches, getting extra cash—or tangible metals such as gold and silver—might not be a bad idea.)

2. *Get your records in order.* Keep good records of all your financial transactions, particularly during the last six months of 1999 and until you receive several bank and brokerage statements in 2000. These records should include documentation of your deposits, investments, ATM withdrawals, and loan payments (credit cards, mortgage, auto loan, etc.). Bank statements and transaction receipts also are among the documents you should be saving.

3. *Reconcile your statements regularly.* This is not the time to toss envelopes in a drawer. Rather, inspect each statement and match checks and deposit receipts with the statement. If you get a credit card statement, make sure your charges and payments are recorded accurately. Contact the bank, brokerage, or charge company immediately if you find any discrepancies.

4. *Be aware of insurance limits on bank accounts.* The FDIC advises people to make sure deposit accounts are within the federal insurance limits, which is always good advice, especially for those with funds in any one insured institution that total more than $100,000. Even if a person has that much on deposit, it's possible under the FDIC's rules to have all these funds fully protected, but the accounts must be set up correctly.

5. *Keep in communication with financial institutions.* Pay special attention to the mailings from your bank and other institutions. These mailings will often include helpful tips. You can—and should—also visit bank and brokerage company Websites. If you have questions or concerns, speak with an employee of your bank who is

knowledgeable about the institution's Y2K program.

6. *Review your loan and credit payment records.* Consider asking lenders and creditors for a printed history of the payments on your mortgage, car loan, or other debts, including how much of each payment has gone toward principal and interest. Check to make sure this history is accurate. (Note that some institutions may charge a fee for these records.)

7. *Look over your credit report.* The FDIC points out that it is always wise to make sure your credit report doesn't contain inaccurate information about your financial reliability. Erroneous information could result in higher interest rates on a loan, a rejection for a job or loan application, or other unnecessary complications. Get a copy of your credit report early in 1999 and if you spot a problem, get it corrected promptly. Then, in 2000, get another copy of your updated report and check again for errors.

To request a copy of your credit report, call the three major credit bureaus at these toll-free numbers: Equifax at (800)685-1111, Experian at (800) 682-7654, and Trans Union at (800)888-4213. Under the Fair Credit Reporting Act there are limits to how much you can be charged for each report ($8 as of late 1998). If you have been denied credit within the past sixty days, you may qualify for a free copy of your report. Remember, credit report information sometimes can vary significantly among the three major credit bureaus, so you may want to request copies from all three companies.

8. *Make sure your personal finance software is Y2K compliant.* Do you use Quicken or Microsoft Money to track your finances? Are you a bank-by-PC fanatic? If you do banking by home computer, contact the computer manufacturer or software vendor to find out if your systems are Y2K-ready. You can find information on Quicken at www.intuit.com and on Microsoft Money at www.microsoft.com/money. Some older versions of Quicken may not be Y2K compliant; in that case, you'll need to upgrade to a newer version and bring your Quicken data over. Also, it's always wise to keep back-up copies of your account records and transactions, perhaps on a removable storage media such as a ZIP cartridge from Iomega. In chapter 7, I will offer a detailed look at how you can prepare your home PC—and its data—for Y2K.

Insurance, the Stock Market, and Y2K

Greater questions surround two other major components of the financial system, the insurance industry and the stock market.

For the insurance industry—life, auto, health, casualty, and property insurance—the questions surrounding Y2K are dual. First is the matter of systems compliance within the insurance firms. If Allstate, for example, could not process a claim, or if State Farm could not issue a check, or if Mutual of Omaha could not monitor premium payments on life insurance—if any of these systems break down, then it becomes impossible for these companies to function and serve customers.

At the same time, a collapse in essential services

under Y2K could result in a barrage of claims flying into insurance companies during the period of the Year 2000 and beyond. If a grocery store loses electricity and thus its food spoils, can that be claimed under an insurance policy? What about a homeowner whose house burns down because a fire truck couldn't be summoned? If traffic lights go out and cars crash, who pays the tab in states where there isn't "no fault" insurance?

According to *BestWeek*, a trade publication covering the insurance industry, "Year 2000 computer repairs could cost the entire U.S. insurance industry a total of $6.58 billion, an estimate based on Y2K disclosures in third-quarter Securities and Exchange Commission filings by the nation's top-60 publicly traded insurers."[9]

Will damage to your home or car because of Y2K problems be covered by your insurance policies? In December 1998, I checked the Websites of three leading insurance companies—Allstate, State Farm, and Farmer's Insurance. None of these companies offered any assurance about coverage for Y2K damage. While this does not mean the companies won't pay on any Y2K claims—policy holders need to read their policies carefully and consult their agents—I would feel more comfortable if these firms offered their usual reassuring words.

For business insurance customers, counting on their commercial property insurance to pay for Y2K-related claims may be risky. In September 1998, the Connecticut State Insurance Department "ruled that insurance policies do not cover costs associated with Year 2000 computer problems unless coverage is specifically stated in the policy," according to an Associated Press dispatch printed in *The Washington Post*.[10]

Wall Street may fare better in Y2K events than many banks or other firms. In July 1998, some twenty-nine securities firms and twelve exchanges simulated trading of stocks and bonds between the last business week of 1999 and the first week of 2000, and the trades passed with flying colors, according to an online report from Wired magazine.[11] An analysis of the tests released in August 1998 by the Securities Industry Association confirmed those results; a final test is due in March 1999.

Applauding the industry, Senator Daniel Patrick Moynihan said, "I am encouraged by the results of these tests conducted by the securities industry. I only hope that the other industries follow the lead of the financial community and start their testing soon. There is no time to waste."[12] Doubtless, millions of investors, savers, and people with insurance are likely to say "Amen" to those words.

Good News on Social Security

Just as this chapter was being finished, some welcome financial news arrived: On December 28, 1998, President Clinton announced that the United States Social Security Administration's payment system had passed rigorous Year 2000 testing.

"The millennium bug will not delay the payment of Social Security checks by a single day," the President said. "The system works, it is secure, and therefore older Americans can feel more secure," he told a White House audience.

It took the Social Security Administration nearly ten years—at a cost of $33 million—to sift through 35 million lines of computer programming code to make the agency Y2K ready. A panel of independent experts verified the results, the agency said.[13]

While payment systems for Medicare and Medicaid

were in doubt at the end of 1998, the word that Social Security would be able to make the 50 million payments it doles out monthly was good news—unless you consider that many of those payments are sent via direct deposit to banks and credit unions, some of which may not be clearing transactions if the Y2K bug hits them.

Endnotes

1. TeleCheck International, Inc. Website (www.telecheck.com) Dec. 1998.

2. Hodges Marshall, letter of 8 Aug. 1998, posted at TeleCheck International, Inc. Website (www.telecheck.com/y2k/merlet1_4.html).

3. Testimony of Ellen Seidman, Senate Y2K Subcommittee, 18 March 1998 (www.senate.gov/banking/98_03hrg/031898/witness/seidman.htm).

4. Quoted in Paul Gentile, "Credit union groups, NCUA plan for potential Y2K-related liquidity shortage," *Credit Union Times*, 23 Dec. 1998, online (www.cutimes.com/y2k/yr121698-1.html).

5. Quoted in NationsBank Website (www.nationsbank.com/y2k/home.htm).

6. NationsBank.

7. "On Track to the Year 2000," Bank of America Website (www.bankamerica.com/batoday/y2k_on-track.html).

8. Some of these ideas were adapted and expanded from a Federal Deposit Insurance Corporation publication, "A Bank Customer's Y2K 'To-Do' List," prepared by Jay Rosenstein of the FDIC's consumer affairs unit, and found at their Website (www.fdic.gov/consumer/consnews/cnfall98/todo.html).

9. Cited in "Insurers' Y2K Costs Could Top $6.58 Billion," *Best-Week*, 14 Dec. 1998.

10. "Connecticut Insurance Dept. Says No Automatic Y2K Coverage," *Washington Post*, 13 Sept. 1998.

11. Yukari Iwatani, "Wall Street Y2K Tests Done," Wired News

online (www.wired.com/news/print_version/business/story/13964.html?wnpg=all) 23 July 1998.

12. Senator Daniel Patrick Moynihan, press statement, 10 Aug. 1998 (www.senate.gov/moynihan/press/y2ktest.htm).

13. Cited in Stephen Barr, "Social Security Killed Y2K Bug, President Says," *Washington Post,* 29 Dec. 1998: A02.

Chapter 5

Planes, Trains, and Automobiles

"Despite [the Federal Aviation Administration's] newfound dedication to fix the Year 2000 problem, the FAA had such a late start that it may not be able to complete the job. While I do not want to be pessimistic about the FAA, I am reminded that a pessimist is simply a well-informed optimist."

—U.S. Rep. Constance A. Morella (R-Md.), House Science Committee, August 8, 1998[1]

Not too long ago, the trucking industry—which hasn't always enjoyed good public relations—adopted a slogan that you might still see on occasion when passing a "big rig" on the highway. "If it came to you, it came by truck," was the essence of that message, and it's the truth, isn't it?

Consider your local supermarket and the trucks that bring to it everything sold in that store. The same goes for other merchants in your community. Sometimes the shipment arrives from a distribution center maintained by the store's owner, such as the Wal-Mart trucks that restock that company's stores. Other times, it's the "less-than-truckload" carriers such as Consolidated Freight-ways that bring individual shipments to several stores in a community. Still other times, it will be the ubiquitous United Parcel Service truck or the one driven by the Federal Express courier. Last—but not least—is the parcel delivery of the U.S. Postal Service, so renowned that once the builder of the Bank of Vernal in Utah shipped the entire bank—brick by brick—from Salt Lake City, using parcel post (authorities later changed the rules on how big a parcel could be to make such shipments less economical than other means of delivery).[2]

All of these means are part of a great, integrated network of transportation, which, like the body's circulatory system, functions often without conscious thought—it just pumps along. You go to the supermarket for a loaf of bread, and it's there. Want a can of heart of palm, which is harvested mostly in Central and South America? Many larger grocers will stock it, which is amazing not only for the variety of food these stores represent, but also for the distance that can had to travel to reach that grocer's shelves.

Like our circulatory system, the transportation network can get snarled sometimes, with difficult results from a blockage. In 1997, a strike by the Teamsters' union against United Parcel Service put 185,000 workers on the street and snarled the delivery of 12 million parcels a day.[3] While other carriers eventually picked up the slack, the strike did lead to some business shutdowns and other difficulties for consumers and entrepreneurs.

The United Parcel Service strike was an event anticipated by all sides and by those with whom UPS competed. When the strike hit, the initial difficulties were somewhat ameliorated by alternative measures, and after the strike was settled, UPS worked diligently to regain lost business. Eighteen months later—as this book goes to press—UPS had one of its best holiday seasons ever, shipping some 430 million packages in the period between Thanksgiving and New Year's Day 1999.

While the UPS strike may be a case of "all's well that ends well," as Shakespeare would say, it also pointed out some of the frailties of the transportation network. On the first day of the UPS walkout, FedEx package volume surged from 2.8 million to over 4 million pieces; handling that amount of traffic required a lot of quick thinking and hard work.

Unlike years gone by, consumers in today's America (and Canada) want and usually receive a wide variety of produce at any time of the year. If a given item of citrus fruit isn't being grown in North America at the time, Brazil, Chile, and Argentina are happy to supply products for U.S. tables—shipped by air, of course, and then delivered by truck. Want roses for Valentine's Day? The bulk of those sold in the U.S. are grown in Colombia, South America, and flown north for the occasion.

Oil and other raw materials come to the U.S. daily via vast cargo ships that prowl the oceans, disgorging their cargo at ports such as New York, New Orleans, Houston, and Long Beach, California. Those ships, in turn, take many American exports back overseas. In 1998, a strike at the Port of Los Angeles left ships in the harbor with precious payloads that could not reach land.

The traffic in goods around the U.S. and between nations should not obscure the millions of people who are on the road each day, shuttling between cities, states, and countries. During the 1999 New Year's weekend alone, some 6 million people were expected to be in transit, numbers that could rise exponentially as millennial revelers fly off to New York, Paris, or Machu Picchu to ring in the next century.

All this, of course, is but a sample of what the transportation system means to us. Whether it's a son or daughter returning from college, a New Zealand-grown leg of lamb for Sunday dinner, or a wedding gift for a niece—having people and things arrive when they're supposed to arrive is at the heart of much of everyday life. Sometimes, such shipments are critical, as is the case with medical supplies or, in the Northeastern United States, heating oil during the winter months.

As this book goes to press, the picture for our planet's transportation networks is mixed. While there are many encouraging signs, there are an equal number that are troublesome.

Should You Fly on January 1, 2000?

One of the biggest questions about the Y2K matter is whether or not it will be safe to fly in an airplane on the first day of the new millennium. Today's aircraft is a computer-controlled marvel. Between takeoff and landing, most jet aircraft require little active control by pilots. Navigational routes are pre-programmed and controls are virtually automatic.

Of course, when unexpected turbulence occurs or course corrections are needed, the skills of pilots come into play, as is the case at takeoff and landing. But from the control panel in the cockpit to the video display system in the cabin, other devices aloft are built on microprocessors and miles and miles of electrical systems.

Moreover, in the United States, it is the Federal Aviation Administration that controls much of the airways. The FAA licenses airlines and pilots, establishes routes for air travel, and maintains the air traffic control network—a team of dedicated, hard-working men and women who keep the airplane traffic evenly spaced around and between airports.

If you are ever near the west side of Los Angeles on a clear night, take a drive along Lincoln Boulevard heading south toward the airport. In the distance, you will notice a dozen or so bright lights, which seem to be hovering in the sky. Drive closer to the airport and you'll realize that these are aircraft, "stacked" and waiting to land on one of the runways at Los Angeles International, or LAX. Air traffic controllers maintain these flight patterns; they view the approaching planes on radar screens and guide each flight in according to a complex series of rules and procedures.

The FAA's air traffic control network consists of one command center and 61 Automated Flight Service Stations (AFSS), 15 Flight Service Stations (FSS), 14 Alaskan Rotational Flight Service Stations, 21 Air Route Traffic Control Centers (ARTCC), 352 Airport Traffic Control Towers (ATCT), 185 Terminal Radar Approach Control (TRACON) facilities, 2 Radar Approach Control (RAPCON) facilities, and 3 Combined Center/Radar Approach Control (CERAP) facilities.[4]

Many of the computer systems that stand behind the air traffic control network are, to put it charitably, a little old. One of these is a network of systems that is *more than twenty years old:* a group of IBM 3080 mainframes called HOST. Though the units are scheduled for replacement before the Year 2000, FAA administrator Jane E. Garvey told the House of Representatives on September 29, 1998, that the agency had patched up the old

IBM system, just in case it's needed:

> With respect to the HOST computer system—one of our core air traffic control systems—with the help of our vendors we have developed a well-defined strategy for the successful transition of the HOST computer into the next century. The existing system is scheduled to be completely replaced by the year 2000. However, as a contingency to HOST replacement, we have already completed renovations of the existing HOST as of July 31, two months ahead of OMB's September 30th renovation deadline. If there is a need for the HOST to be operational in the Year 2000, we are assured that it will transition to the new millennium in a routine manner.[5]

That patch couldn't come soon enough: On August 19, 1998, the IBM mainframe used at the FAA's New England regional control center crashed, stranding planes on the ground for thirty-eight minutes as controllers passed scraps of paper between them to track flights already airborne. The cause? Possibly a "bad data interface," according to one account.[6]

While the FAA's Garvey says that all elements of the U.S. air traffic control system will be Year 2000 compliant by June 30, 1999, there are those who doubt that all will truly be well. It is currently impossible to judge whether the FAA will meet its goals, although the agency has won praise from some congressional overseers for their determination.

Even the most determined of plans can fail. According to Garvey's House testimony, there is some disagreement over what will happen in the air:

Although I am pleased with and proud of the progress that the FAA has made in solving our Y2K problems, we do recognize that Y2K presents a set of problems we have never encountered before, and that there are differing views as to how those problems should be defined and solved. We also recognize that different stakeholders will have widely ranging resources and expertise in solving Y2K problems. The FAA is committed to doing whatever we can within the scope of our authority to assist the members of the aviation industry to make a smooth transition to the new millennium.[7]

Echoing her overall optimism, FAA administrator Garvey said she would be on an airplane when the clocks roll over at midnight on December 31, 1999.[8] Similar sentiments have been expressed by John Koskinen, the top Clinton Administration official overseeing the Y2K bug: He plans to board a commercial flight from New York to Washington on January 1, 2000.

Others in the field have different plans. James R. (Randy) Schwitz, executive vice president of the National Air Traffic Controllers Association, the union representing controllers, told CNN he will be at home on New Year's Day 2000: "I, for one, will not be flying, and I will not let my family fly," he said.[9] The union has blasted FAA efforts to rectify issues involving the HOST system, claiming that IBM has told agency officials the computer firm "does not have 'the appropriate skills and tools' to debug the machines because they are more than twenty years old. Thus, IBM will not guarantee all errors will be found, much less corrected by Dec. 31, 1999."[10]

It isn't merely the air traffic controllers union that is expressing concern about the FAA's Year 2000 readiness. The U.S. General Accounting Office, which audits the performance of federal agencies, is also concerned about the FAA's approach. Joel C. Willemssen, who directs the GAO's Civil Agencies Information Systems office, told the House of Representatives at the August 6, 1998, hearing of three main concerns:

> FAA's projections for completing renovation, validation, and implementation of mission-critical systems show that the Agency will not meet OMB's milestones. For example, only 61 percent of mission-critical systems needing repair are expected to be implemented by the March 1999 deadline. . . .
>
> Second, FAA's projections are based on very optimistic schedules that may not be realistic. For example, as of July 31st [1998], just 4 of 159 mission-critical systems needing repair had been implemented. The FAA projects that this number will increase to 46 by next February and one month later, in March of 1999, more than double to 97. . . .
>
> In addition, after testing at the technical centers, many of the systems must be then tested and implemented at numerous sites across the country. A task of this complexity will be time-consuming and difficult. FAA must also test its critical business processes and supporting systems end-to-end. FAA will need a significant amount of time to do this.[11]

Major U.S.-based airlines are working quickly to get ready for the Year 2000. According to a December 17, 1998, statement, United Air Lines is nearing completion of its Y2K preparations:

United Airlines has had an intensive, proactive Year 2000 project underway since 1995 to address every facet of its global operation, and with a goal of providing safe, uninterrupted service to customers on Jan. 1, 2000, and beyond. So far, United's Y2K team has investigated more than 14,600 items as part of its technical assessment of the company's computer systems and computer-driven equipment.[12]

The airline expects all its systems to be Year 2000 ready by no later than June 30, 1999. "We're reaching out to share information and form common solutions," the airline's Y2K project director, Rick Juster, said in the news release. "In fact, airline manufacturers Boeing and Airbus have already assured us their aircraft have no safety or flight issues. We want airline travelers to feel confident that United—and the industry—will be ready."[13]

One prominent member of the airline industry may not share United's stated enthusiasm. According to CNN Financial News Correspondent Kelli Arena, "One airline—KLM Royal Dutch—says it may not fly on January 1, because many governments have been too late to respond to the problem."[14] There have also been unconfirmed reports that the FAA will issue a "quarantine list" of international airports which may not be Y2K compliant.

Globally, the International Civil Aviation Organization, ICAO, a United Nations agency, is responsible for coordinating air safety efforts among the world's nations. According to ICAO spokesman Vincent Gallotti, "We feel that we have to continue to raise awareness. I think the . . . threat has not fully materialized yet, but it is becoming materialized now, and as that threat materializes, I think that we'll see more clearly where the problem areas are."[15]

Should you be on an airplane when January 1, 2000, rolls around? At this writing, it's too early for me to give an unqualified Yes answer; this is clearly a situation that bears close scrutiny as 1999 unfolds.

Railroads, Highways, and Ports

Of considerable interest to many people are the questions of what is likely to happen in the areas of rail and highway transportation, as well as ocean shipping. Those goods that you receive via truck travel on a highway, before that may have been moved by rail. In addition, some 95 percent of America's foreign trade comes via ship.

On October 2, 1998, the House Committee on Transportation and Infrastructure held one of a series of hearings on the Year 2000 situation. There, Linda J. Morgan, chairman of the Surface Transportation Board that oversees America's rail system, gave this assessment of the rail network, based on a 1997 survey:

> We concluded that the railroad industry had made significant progress in developing and implementing plans to eliminate any Year 2000 malfunctions that could threaten service or safety. . . . In response to this survey, all of the major railroads indicated that all of their systems would be able to deal with the changeover to 2000.[16]

Four days later, Gloria Jeff, deputy administrator of the Federal Highway Administration, told the same panel that any Year 2000 disruptions on the road would be more of an inconvenience than a breakdown of mass proportions:

The initial assessments by [the] States have indicated a small number of problems may cause inefficient operation of traffic signals if left uncorrected. Actions to address these inefficiencies are being undertaken. The States of Washington and Minnesota have been leaders in this area. . . . Embedded chips are commonly used in traffic control devices. Our outreach efforts have emphasized the importance of assessing the impact of Y2K on mainframe as well as embedded technology. To date, we have determined that chip failures will not present traffic safety problems. If errors occur, signals will operate properly, but inefficiently.[17]

Behind these sanguine assessments of the situation, however, there are some concerns. At the October 6th hearing, Kathy Hofstedt, Year 2000 project manager for the Minnesota Department of Transportation (Mn/DOT), told representatives of her concerns about the millennium:

Mn/DOT's greatest exposure appears to be in determining the Year 2000 progress of its suppliers and business partners. . . . For example, Mn/DOT is dependent on electric utilities to provide electricity for traffic control signals; petroleum companies to provide fuel for its snow plows, sand and salt trucks; and telecommunications for its emergency dispatch system. Five potential areas of vulnerability for Mn/DOT are public utilities, trucking industry, railroads, U.S. DOT and cities and counties. . . . In August, 1998, Mn/DOT sent out a survey to 945 of its most critical suppliers to have them confirm their Year 2000 readiness. To date 70 percent have not responded to the survey. In addition,

The Minnesota Department of Public Service surveyed 317 electric, natural gas, telecommunication and pipeline utilities doing business in Minnesota. Fifty percent of the respondents said they did not have a Year 2000 project team in place to examine the effect Year 2000 will have on their companies.[18]

For the railroads, the outlook is more hopeful, even though that light at the end of the tunnel may yet prove to be an oncoming locomotive. Consider the statements of Joyce Wrenn, vice president of information technology and chief information officer for Union Pacific Railroad. The carrier, she admits, is one of the nation's most important: "Union Pacific is the largest railroad in the country, operating 36,000 miles of track in 23 states."[19]

Given the size of the railroad, it's not surprising that Union Pacific is a technology driven company: "We are dependent on 72 million lines of code in mainframe systems, over 100 newer client/server applications with 8 million lines of code, and millions of daily EDI transactions with customers, vendors and other railroads plus services from hundreds of service providers."[20]

While 80 percent of Union Pacific's mainframe systems had been certified as Y2K compliant by September 1998 (the balance due by the end of that year), Wrenn reported that only 30 percent of the railroad's client-server systems had been so certified.[21] The balance were due to be ready no later than 1999, she said, but a breakdown in desktop information systems could spell trouble for the rail line, which has had other major problems in years past, including some tragic—and traffic-stopping—derailments and other capacity headaches.

"Despite our best efforts, we recognize that total coverage of all Y2K internal and external problems is unlikely," Wrenn said. "Currently, we plan to have a Y2K command center staffed 24 hours a day in the fourth quarter of 1999 and continuing into early 2000 for any problems that might occur due to the Y2K."[22]

Along with rail traffic, disruption of ocean-borne commerce could also create headaches. According to Rear Admiral George N. Nacarra of the United States Coast Guard, severe problems may result:

> The United States economy is extraordinarily dependent upon maritime shipping. . . . I only need mention that according to the Energy Information Administration, more than 50 percent of the oil consumed in this country comes to us from foreign sources through our ports. Add to this the fact that 95 percent of all the overseas cargo entering the U.S. comes via our ports, and over 97 percent of that comes in foreign ships. Any disruption of the cargo and especially oil flow, for even a few days, would have a discernible effect on our economy, particularly during the winter heating season.[23]

In December, 1998, Nacarra said the Coast Guard may have to stop oil tankers from trying to unload in U.S. ports on December 31, 1999, and later, if the ships aren't Y2K compliant.[24]

The Bottom Line: What Will Be Moving?

By now, readers should sense a pattern in the public discussion of Year 2000 issues. There is one group which claims (or hopes) that no serious disruptions will occur, even though some (such as the Union Pacific Railroad) are setting up contingency plans just in case. On the other side, there are those raising serious alarm, such as James R. (Randy) Schwitz of the National Air Traffic Controllers Association.

On the roads, there are concerns if you listen to officials such as Kathy Hofstedt of the Minnesota Department of Transportation. While it is clear that highways will not crumble into dust on January 1, 2000, the systems that support the smooth and efficient movement of road and rail traffic across the country might be affected. If traffic lights do not work, if toll collections cannot be made, if drawbridges cannot open or close, and tunnels are dark, the potential for accidents and disruptions may be great. And, since much of America's raw materials, food, and manufactured goods move by rail, the smooth functioning of that system—along with the highways used by truck carriers—will be vital. However, progress is continuing, and so it is quite possible that by New Year's Eve only a few systems will remain vulnerable to the bug and so most travel will continue without a hitch.

Endnotes

1. Statement of Representative Constance A. Morella, Chair, Technology Subcommittee of House Science Committee, 8 Aug. 1998.

2. "The Bank That Broke the Mailman's Back," 1973 ed., *Old Farmer's Almanac,* p. 152.

3. "Teamsters strike after UPS talks fail: Deliveries to thousands threatened," *The Dallas Morning News,* 4 Aug. 1997: 1A.

4. FAA Air Traffic Service Website (www.faa.gov/ats/at.htm).

5. Jane F. Garvey, testimony, House of Representatives, 29 Sept. 1998 (www.house.gov/transportation/y2k/garvey.htm).

6. Frank Tiboni, "New England Air Traffic Control Systems Crash," *Government Computer News,* 31 Aug. 1998 (www.ntgov.com/gcn/gcn/1998/august31/8a.htm).

7. Garvey.

8. Steve Young, "Countdown to the Millennium Bug," Cable News Network, 1 Jan. 1999 (www.cnn.com/TRANSCRIPTS/9901/01/se.01.html).

9. Young.

10. "Year 2000 Fact Sheet," National Air Traffic Controllers Association (home.natca.org/natca/mediaandpublicrelations/2000.html).

11. Willemssen, report to the House of Representatives, 6 Aug. 1998, online (www.house.gov/science/willemssen_08-06.htm).

12. United Air Lines, "Year 2000 Team Working At Full Speed," news release, 17 Dec. 1998 (www.ual.com/asp/press_view_detail_print.asp?rec_nbr=429).

13. United Air Lines.

14. Young.

15. Young.

16. Linda J. Morgan, statement, House of Representatives, 2 Oct. 1998 (www.house.gov/transportation/y2k/morgan.htm).

17. Gloria Jeff, testimony, House of Representatives, 6 Oct. 1998 (www.house.gov/transportation/y2k/jeff.htm).

18. Testimony of Kathy Hofstedt, House of Representatives, 6 Oct. 1998 (www.house.gov/transportation/y2k/hofstedt.htm).

19. Testimony of Joyce Wrenn, Senate Y2K Committee, 10 Sept. 1998 (www.senate.gov/y2k/statements/091098wrenn.html).

20. Wrenn.

21. Wrenn.

22. Wrenn.

23. Testimony of Rear Admiral George N. Nacarra, House of Representatives, 7 Oct. 1998 (www.house.gov/transportation/y2k/naccara.htm).

24. Bob Brewin and Orlando DeBruce, "Coast Guard Raises Y2K Warning Flag," *Federal Computer Week,* 7 Dec. 1998 (www.fcw.com/pubs/fcw/1998/1207/fcw-newscoast-12-7-98.html).

Chapter 6

A Millennium
of Moment--
or of Madness?

When we were children, we were in slavery under
the basic principles of the world. But when the time
had fully come, God sent his Son, born of a woman,
born under law, to redeem those under law, that we
might receive the full rights of sons.

Galatians 4:3-5

It is truly amazing and ironic that as the world sits
on the precipice of a new millennium, with all its
technology, know-how, and sophistication, this
small matter of how many digits were assigned to
the year dates in computer code could cause such
uncertainty and fear.

Dr. William J. Hamel, President, Evangelical Free Church of America[1]

Looking at the Scripture above, and contrasting it with
the comment from Dr. Hamel, one is struck that there
may be two ways in which the Year 2000 unfurls for
believers. Will this be a year of great moment or one of
great madness?

Both outcomes are possible. If the worst technological breakdowns occur or if widespread panic erupts, some level of madness in society could result. If things proceed more smoothly, then the spiritual events of the Year 2000 may end up being the most memorable of all.

Before discussing what some leading Christian groups are doing to mark the arrival of the third millennium, let's look at some of the reasons why there is so great a focus in the public mind about this particular year, and what the dawning of a new millennium may represent to spiritual seekers.

Don't Stop Thinking about Tomorrow

For almost as long as I could remember, my generation—seemingly more than any other—was being propelled towards the future. Perhaps it comes from being born at the time of the first orbital satellite, Sputnik, in 1957. The "race for space" that followed pitted the best scientists of the United States and the then-Soviet Union in a fierce competition to see who could put a man on the moon first. The U.S. won that race in 1969; five years later, American and Soviet space travelers docked ships and shook hands thousands of miles above the surface of the planet. Today, as I write, the first elements of an international space station are in orbit, again a joint venture between the United States and what is now Russia.

My own experience of being focused on the future came from growing up near the site of the 1964 World's Fair in Flushing Meadows, New York. There, we saw exhibits of the AT&T "Picturephone," which combined a television camera and telephone in what seemed like a fantastic vision of communications. (Now you can achieve a similar effect, at far lower cost, with a small video camera, a desktop computer and modem, an Internet connection, and software.)

Also during the 1960s, much of the world experienced a ferment not seen since perhaps the Second World War. Brazil, the largest nation in South America, moved from democracy to military dictatorship, under which it would languish for more than two decades. The streets of Paris flowed with the blood of student protesters, calling on the Gaullist government to move toward the left. In Czechoslovakia, a "Prague spring" of political reform was crushed by the invasion of Soviet troops. In Mainland China, the "Cultural Revolution" unleashed hordes of Red Guards on the populace, stamping out any thought that deviated from the teachings of Chinese communist leader Mao Zedong. The Six-Day War rocked the Middle East in 1967 when Israel retook Jerusalem and forced the once-proud Egyptian army into a hurried retreat across the Sinai desert.

In America, debate and dissension over the Vietnam War tore the country apart, while racial conflicts in the South helped ignite riots in Los Angeles, Newark, and Detroit. The assassination of President John F. Kennedy in 1963, the Reverend Dr. Martin Luther King, Jr., in April, 1968, and Sen. Robert F. Kennedy two months later all contributed to a sense of national unease. During those days, visions of a brighter future were held out as something to look forward to after the difficult days had passed.

But the end of the 1960s didn't mean the end of national unrest in America. In the 1970s, the muddle of Vietnam, the 1973 energy crisis and Mideast war, and the Watergate affair surrounding President Richard M.

Nixon further divided and distressed many. It was during this time that speakers on Bible prophecy such as Hal Lindsay and Pat Robertson began to sound the call to a return of Jesus Christ and the end of the current era. Such calls were not limited to the Protestant/evangelical arena: In Brooklyn, New York, followers of the Lubavitcher Rebbe, Rabbi Menachem Mendel Schneerson, began advertising on signs and bumper stickers, "We want Moshiach now!" calling for the promised Jewish messiah.

Apart from the geopolitical morass in which so much of the world found itself, there were tremendous advances in science, medicine, and technology. The space program spurred computer development and deployment; it also gave us Teflon-coated cookware and freeze-dried foods. South African surgeon Dr. Christiaan Barnard performed the world's first heart transplant. And satellite communications—another happy byproduct of the space race—brought the world closer together, allowing real time images of faraway events to arrive on home television screens.

Looming over all of this for decades—from about 1945 to 1989, in fact—was the specter of nuclear war and the destruction that would follow. The 1983 television movie, *The Day After,* presented in chilling detail a vision of what might happen during such a cataclysm. The picture was not a pretty one, and for decades people in Europe and America campaigned for disarmament, even if it was unilateral. The end of the Soviet Union and collapse of the Berlin Wall at the end of the 1980s was the start of a transformational decade that brought America, and much of the world, unbridled prosperity and advancement. By the end of the 1990s, the rise of online communications and the explosive growth of the Internet—and a concurrent jump in American stock market values—helped create a feeling of optimism that replaced the fears of earlier periods.

For me and millions like me all these events had us turned towards the future, looking for what was around the corner. During the height of the Cold War, many found comfort in various prophetic interpretations. (A favorite indoor sport in many fundamentalist quarters was to "pin the tail on the Antichrist," as author and pastor William M. Alnor put it[2]). Others sought in science and technology salvation either in real life by being involved in these industries, or through escapist science fiction such as the famed *Star Trek* series. The burgeoning interest in UFOs and close encounters—e.g., *The X Files*, with its claim that "the truth is out there" is another symbol, I believe, of a massive search for what lies beyond this present age and its troubles.[3]

A Countdown to Tomorrow's World

Thus it should be no surprise that millions of people are viewing the advent of the Year 2000 as something more than just the turning of a calendar page. Around the world, religious organizations are planning numerous events to welcome the next millennium—even if there's some disagreement on just when the millennium is to begin.

Of course, much of this speculation is limited to the greater Christian world. For Jews, next year will be the year 5760 (their Year 2000 was our 1762 B.C.). For Muslims, what the West considers the Year 2000 will begin as the last part of 1420 A.H. (or after *hijirah* when, Muslims teach, the Messenger Mohammed migrated from Makkah to Medina, cutting relations with his former tribe).

Indeed, for the Western world, the first day of the new millennium might actually have been the fourteenth day of the last month of the old, depending upon which calendar system is used. Originally, the Roman Emperor Julius Caesar created the Julian calendar in 46 B.C. as a modified form of the old Roman republican calendar, which was based on lunar cycles. The new Julian calendar set fixed lengths for the months, abandoning the lunar cycle. It also specified that there would be exactly twelve months per year and 365.25 days per year with every fourth year being a leap year.

In reality, however, the length of a "tropical" year, i.e., one measured at the equator, is 365.242199 days. The discrepancy wreaked havoc on dates (at one point, in some places in England, it could be any of three different dates!) and it also messed up the arrival of the spring equinox, which hurt agriculture. In 1582, Pope Gregory XIII sought to even out the matter by decreeing that Thursday, October 4 of that year would be followed by Friday, October 15. Centennial years would be a leap year only if they were a multiple of 400. This shortened the year by three days per 400 years, giving a year of 365.2425 days—not as precise as the tropical year, but a bit more accurate and one that kept the equinox in its place.

As if all this wasn't confusing enough, there are some who suggest that the millennium—if it is defined as the 2000th anniversary year of the birth of Jesus Christ—has actually passed us by, virtually unnoticed. Some scholars, trying to fix the location and reason for the famed Star of Bethlehem, search astronomical history and then calculate the actual date of Jesus' birth as taking place in what we would consider 3 B.C. Others say it was 5 B.C. or even 7 B.C. At the low end of this scale, it would mean that the real millennium arrived in 1998.[4] (And to think you didn't have the appropriate party!)

Such speculations aside, the fact is that much of the Christian world, if not all of it, will view the arrival of January 1, 2000, as a significant milestone in history. Among the events scheduled for the Year 2000 are those described in the following pages, which by no means is a comprehensive list but a representative sampling of what many Christians are planning.

Jubilee 2000

The world's largest Christian group (just under 976 million adherents[5]), the Roman Catholic Church, has seen its leader, Pope John Paul II proclaim this event as Jubilee 2000. In an exhortation titled "On The Coming Of The Third Millennium," the pope said this to his church's faithful:

> The whole Church is invited, through three years of preparation, to open the door to the third millennium by opening the doors of our hearts to the trinity, and especially to Jesus Christ. Therefore, this preparation is primarily a *journey to deepen our spiritual life*—to be the holy people God calls us to be.[6]

The Catholic Church, both in the United States and around the world, is using the Year 2000 as a keynote for many events. Special congresses will be held in Rome and in other centers, with an emphasis on the church's sacraments, particularly the Sacrament of Reconciliation, and there are active hopes that Pope John Paul II will be able to visit various holy sites in Israel and the Palestinian-controlled West Bank during that year.

In addition, the pope has written of a desire for a more ecumenical conference, under Vatican auspices:

> The ecumenical and universal character of the Sacred Jubilee can be fittingly reflected by a meeting of all Christians. This would be an event of great significance, and so, in order to avoid misunderstandings, it should be properly presented and carefully prepared, in an attitude of fraternal cooperation with Christians of other denominations and traditions, as well as of grateful openness to those religions whose representatives might wish to acknowledge the joy shared by all the disciples of Christ.[7]

Amsterdam 2000

On July 29, 2000, an expected group of 10,000 itinerant evangelists will meet at the RAI Conference Center in Amsterdam for an historic conference. Called Amsterdam 2000 for its location in The Netherlands and the millennium year in which it will occur, the Billy Graham Evangelistic Association (BGEA) is sponsoring the conference. Graham, who has preached the gospel to more people than any other living person, will be general chairman of the event.

"The Billy Graham organization is the only one in the world that can put on a conference of this size," said Richard Bewes, Rector of All Souls Anglican Church in London and a member of the international program-planning group. "The confidence is there. Billy Graham is known for integrity."

Two individuals selected by Graham lead the international committee planning the event. They are Dr. John

Corts, president and chief operation officer of the BGEA, who is general director of Amsterdam 2000, and Dr. John Akers, program chairman and a special assistant to Billy Graham for research and special projects. Both Corts and Akers are ordained ministers with over twenty years experience with the Graham organization.

According to the organizers, who met in Los Angeles at the end of 1998 to map out plans for the event:

> The year 2000 represents a historic opportunity to present the unchanging truth of Jesus Christ against a backdrop of dramatic social and technological change worldwide. On a personal level, they were also aware that Billy Graham, at age 80, has a deep sense of conviction about equipping and encouraging the next generation to carry on the work of evangelism with a high degree of integrity. . . .
>
> The moral and ethical decay of our times leaves a tremendous gap in leadership in the world. There is an urgency to blend our heartbeat to walk with God into the next century. We want everyone to know that Amsterdam 2000 is not just a subject for the religion media; it has an all pervasive application to how we live and what we do.[8]

Edwin Martinez, a Latin American evangelist and a Graham associate, added: "There is momentum as we approach the year 2000. People have an excitement and expectation that something is going to happen. The expectation is creating a void in people's hearts. The opportunity for evangelists is to fill the void with Christ."

Logistics for this event are likely to be immense. Among the responsibilities of the program staff is interpretation of conference sessions and materials into twenty-five or more languages, the organizers noted.[9] This Amsterdam 2000 event will come seventeen years after the 1983 International Congress for Itinerant Evangelists, which was also held in that city.

AD2000 & Beyond

The AD2000 & Beyond Movement "seeks to encourage cooperation in establishing a church within every unreached people group and making the gospel available to every person by the year 2000," according to a statement.[10] The AD2000 & Beyond Movement has spread the vision for reaching the "10/40 Window," a geographic region first identified by the Movement's International Director, Luis Bush. The 10/40 Window is the rectangular area of North Africa, the Middle East and Asia between 10 degrees north and 40 degrees north latitude where 99 percent of the world's least-evangelized poor are found. The AD2000 prayer initiative, called "Praying Through the Window" has mobilized over 30 million intercessors worldwide to pray for people who live in the 10/40 Window.

In addition, the movement will sponsor a "Celebrate Jesus 2000" conference in Jerusalem that will take place at the *end* of the year 2000 and going into the first days of 2001.

Mission America and Celebrate Jesus 2000

Separately, the Mission America organization will sponsor a "Celebrate Jesus 2000" campaign as "a rallying point for Christians to come together to pray for and share Christ with every person in America," the group said.[11] Along with prayer and personal witness—the goal being to reach every American household by the Year 2000—Mission America also plans larger scale evangelistic efforts:

> Partnership areas will plan for "proclamation" activities—public events where the Gospel is proclaimed. These proclamation activities will vary from community to community and may include area-wide or local church evangelistic crusades. Other ideas include multi-media campaigns, drama and Christian concerts. . . . It is projected that in the fall of 1999, a concluding national event for the proclamation component would be a coordinated satellite transmission of an evangelistic crusade by a recognized and respected national evangelist. Other national programs with specialized emphases will provide additional opportunities for proclamation evangelism.[12]

Mission America is also keeping an eye on the Year 2000 situation in terms of potential impact on society. In late 1998, the organization convened a meeting in Colorado Springs to help plan for disaster response. According to Dr. Cornell Haan, who is heading up the group's Y2K efforts, "We wanted to look at what the church should do relative to evangelism; this could be the greatest opportunity we have seen in our current history. How can the church be prepared should there be some disruption?"[13]

Lutheran Church--Missouri Synod 3-10 Campaign

According to Rev. Paul McCain, assistant to the president, the Lutheran Church Missouri Synod with 6,200 U.S. congregations and 2.6 million members is focusing more on outreach in the Year 2000 than on stockpiling supplies. McCain said the church will "[use the] last three years of our old millennium to prepare for the first ten years of the new," by engaging in evangelism training and outreach. He said the goal of the "3-10" program is to prepare church members for "an unprecedented outreach from our church."[14]

"From 1998 to 2001, these years will be an intentional process of growth in evangelism issues," McCain told me. "From 2001 for the next ten years, we'll have an unprecedented outreach from our church." He said that the evangelization will embrace the entire denomination, long known for its conservative theological stance and its "Lutheran Hour" broadcast: "We want to involve our whole church in a large outreach effort. We're finding, frankly, that the message of our church—a conservative, Biblical message—is more attractive."[15]

Salvation Army International Millennial Congress

From every corner of the globe, members of the unique branch of the Christian church called The Salvation Army will gather in Atlanta, Georgia, in July 2000 for "The Army Next," an International Millennial Congress. This event will feature much pageantry and musical expression along with a powerful presentation of the gospel message. (I'll admit a bias here: The Army is my church home.) The Army statement notes that it

> is called to fight a wide variety of battles for the Lord, and in order to achieve victory it must be

remade on a daily basis in the thoughts, prayers, and plans of those who call themselves Salvationists. Thus, if we truly want to see spiritual victories in the days to come, we should be looking ahead to the next step in our ministry, anticipating the next challenge and relying fully upon the power of the Holy Spirit. We should look to the future and consciously choose to make the Army a more powerful force for God. . . .

Admittedly, such an approach might mean change, and we must therefore be willing to update our strategies. But the simple fact is that we must move forward, not only because the alternative is stagnation and defeat, and certainly not because our plans are flawless or our people perfect, but because the message we proclaim commands it.[16]

Jubilee 2000 Debt Relief

The Jubilee 2000 movement, headquartered in London, is based on the Old Testament principle of Jubilee. As noted in Leviticus 25:10, each fiftieth year was to be celebrated as a Jubilee Year when slaves were to be released and land was to be returned to original owners so that families would have the opportunity for a fresh start. (Land in Israel was not to be sold for good. Instead, land was owned by the family, or tribe, to which it was originally given in the division of the Promised Land. When a family was in debt and had to "sell" land, it was sold for the years remaining until the Jubilee Year. Then with the Jubilee the land would be returned to the original family, thus preventing the destitution of one family or tribe and enrichment of another.)

Many developing nations experienced great burdens

in the 1980s as major economic powers raised interest rates to control their own economies. As those indebted countries ran into difficulties, they sought help from the International Monetary Fund (IMF) or the World Bank. The IMF with the World Bank imposed conditions on those countries to improve their economies in exchange for additional loans. These conditions, known as Structural Adjustment Programs, have often meant reductions in basic services. Higher prices for basic goods, fewer opportunities for education, and a lower level of health care spending have made life difficult and oppressive at the grass-roots level. (Different IMF conditions are now being imposed on nations such as South Korea and Brazil as these nations seek to reorganize their economies.)

The Jubilee 2000 Coalition is engaged in lobbying decision makers in various governments, international financial institutions, and other important bodies, and it has established an important network of supporters who share its objectives. The Coalition believes that the oppression of Third World debt could be ended by the year 2000. Then the world could begin the new millennium with new hope for poor nations, and a new start for international relations.

The main action of the Jubilee 2000 Coalition at present has been gathering signatures for a global "Jubilee 2000 Petition" (which they hope will be the world's largest). They handed in 1.5 million signatures at the Group of Eight Industrialized Nations (or G8) Summit in Birmingham in 1998 and plan to hand in the next installment at the 1999 G8 Summit, due to be held in Germany.[17] It is unclear how the IMF and members of the G8 will react, although there has been no acceptance by any major country as yet.

As the Year 2000 approaches, and doubtless throughout that year and into 2001, there will be a number of creative celebrations engaged in by the Christian world, both to mark the passing of another millennium and to remind the world at large just why there is a celebration in the first place. Only time will tell whether that world at large will note those events more clearly than any computer disruptions.

Endnotes

1. William J. Hamel, "Pastoral Letter to EFCA Pastors and Leaders Regarding Y2K," Evangelical Free Church of America, 18 Dec. 1998 (www.efca.org/y2k.html).

2. William M. Alnor, *Soothsayers of the Second Advent* (Baker Book House, 1989).

3. See also William M. Alnor, *UFO Cults and the New Millennium* (Baker Book House, 1998) in which he argues the current wave of UFO mania is inspired in part by a Hollywood fixation on the subject.

4. See, for example, Robert Cooke, "A Little Puzzle Of Bethlehem Scientists still search for explanation of the Christmas Star," *Newsday*, 22 Dec. 1992: 51 for a discussion of various dates for the appearance of the star and, thus, differing estimates of the actual year of Jesus' birth.

5. *1998 Catholic Almanac,* as quoted by the National Conference of Catholic Bishops of the United States, Jubilee 2000 Website (www.nccbuscc.org/jubilee/resources/stats.htm).

6. Pope John Paul II, "Tertio Millennio Adveniente," quoted by the National Conference of Catholic Bishops of the United States, 1998 (www.nccbuscc.org/jubilee/whoweare.htm#vision).

7. Pope John Paul II. (www.vatican.va/jubilee_2000/documents/enframe0_en.htm).

8. Information and quotes on Amsterdam 2000 from news release, 16 Dec. 1998 (www.amsterdam2000.org/NewsAnnouncement2.asp).

9. News release, Amsterdam 2000.

10. "AD2000 and Beyond Movement Overview," Feb. 1996 (www.ad2000.org/ad2kbroc.htm).

11. Source, Mission America Website (www.missionamerica.org/cj2000.html).

12. Mission America Website.

13. Dr. Cornell Haan, telephone interview, 25 Nov. 1998.

14. Rev. Paul McCain, quoted in Kellner, "Y2K—A Secular Apocalypse?" *Christianity Today*, 11 Jan. 1999.

15. Reverend McCain, telephone interview, 9 Nov. 1998.

16. News release, "The Army Next—Carrying the Flame into the Future," 3 July 1998 (www.sarmy.org/intnews.nsf/08af486696be85cb802566210045618c/17f0c6a866acbea0802566360048020a?OpenDocument).

17. Adapted and expanded from Salvation Army, International News Release, 15 Sept. 1998 (www.sarmy.org/intnews.nsf/08af486696be85cb802566210045618c/497213f22779709780256677f00523d1e?OpenDocument).

Chapter 7

Quick Fixes at Church, Work, and Home

Be very careful, then, how you live—not as unwise but as wise, making the most of every opportunity, because the days are evil. Therefore do not be foolish, but understand what the Lord's will is.

Ephesians 5:15-17

So, what should you do about all this? What should I do? How can we "make the most of every opportunity"—as Paul told the band of believers at Ephesus who weren't even close to worrying about the Year 100? What can we do between now and December 31, 1999, to make sure of the stability of equipment and services for the following day and the following year?

As in many circumstances, the key is knowledge and understanding. There's a reason that Solomon, in Proverbs 4:7 (KJV), asserts that his reader should "get wisdom: and with all thy getting get understanding." Knowing the latest about the Year 2000 situation is the key to securing those things that are under your immediate influence. That's why you are reading this book. And if you've just opened the book to this chapter, please go back and at least glance over the earlier chapters so you can get an understanding of what is happening and why.[1]

Along with that knowledge and understanding, there are specific things that can be done to make sure that conditions at church, at home, and at work are a little easier. Let's start with your church. Whether you are the pastor, a deacon, or just a congregant, the church is an important part of your life that could face serious disruption in a Y2K meltdown.

To some extent, all these suggestions are interrelated: If you are responsible for the administration of a church, you will want to review the suggestions made for businesses as well, not to mention those for your home; those primarily concerned about a home probably work in a business and attend a church. So, look at all three sections to get a full-orbed view of the Y2K situation.

Solutions for Your Church[2]

For a moment—and only for a moment—forget that your church is a center for preaching the gospel. Instead, think about the systems used to run a building (or a complex of buildings) which serves a large number of people each week. In North America, many churches run on the same systems that a small or medium-sized business uses. And just as your insurance agent, your realtor, or your attorney's offices may collapse, so too might the systems which keep your sanctuary a, well, sanctuary for your congregation.

A church is in effect a business. Financial records and membership records are stored on church computers, as is vital correspondence. Clearly these systems are significant, though perhaps not as significant as other systems.

Using a program such as Norton 2000, you should check out your PCs for Y2K problems with the BIOS, or Basic Input/Output System, chip that tells the PC things like the date and what it means. Then, follow the recommendations the software gives for updating programs and data files. Updates will be available from the Symantec Website.

If your PCs are on a network, it's important to work with your network system vendor (Novell, Microsoft, etc.) to make sure you have the latest version of their software that is Y2K compliant. Then, check to ensure it is installed and working properly. The same obviously applies to church management software vendors. Again, check Websites for information on Y2K compliance, or get it in writing from the people who sold you the software.

It's also imperative that you gain assurances from your banks and other financial partners that their systems are Y2K compliant so that your accounts are in order after the fateful date. Another good idea here would be to follow the basic ideas discussed in chapter 4 for safeguarding bank and other investment accounts: verify with your financial institutions, keep printouts of the last six months' records, and perhaps have some cash on hand for emergency spending.

The greater issue for most churches, however, may well be in the area of embedded systems. The devices which control heating, lighting, audio, refrigeration— each of these *could* be affected, although it's difficult to know which systems will be. That's because, according to estimates, there are some 50 *billion* embedded systems chips in use worldwide. Some are date sensitive, some are not. As with society in general, your church could be involved in a "roll of the dice" come January 1, 2000.

Handling these embedded systems could be tricky at best. Your survival tactic here may be to work with service personnel from each of the companies which made or supplied these systems and see if a test can be run that won't shut down your operation. (Another suggestion might be to roll back the clock on these devices to 1972, which matches 2000 date for date, down to the day of the week.)

In the best of cases, your systems will pass with flying colors. In the worst, some may need to be replaced, which will be an additional drain on capital reserves. But it's better to know this as far in advance of the Y2K event as possible than to be surprised when it hits.

According to Y2K experts, there are two chief things a church can do to prepare for possible disruptions in service due to Y2K. One is to become a proactive consumer. Demand that your suppliers—particularly the utilities—have systems in place to continue service. One voice may or may not move a giant utility, but the consistent voices of you and your parishioners can make a difference, as David Yonggi Cho, pastor of the world's largest congregation, the 350,000-member Yoido Full Gospel Church in Seoul, Korea, well knows. Needing a loan to buy some land, Pastor Cho went to the head of a bank and asked whether the institution would give a loan if he, Cho, would bring 50,000 new accounts to the bank. The officer agreed, Pastor Cho gave the word in Sunday services, and the next Monday the bank had 50,000 new customers.

The other thing to do to prepare is to meet the needs of those individuals who are unable or unwilling to prepare for the worst. In times of crisis, Christian churches can be lights in their communities. With the potential for disruption that Y2K brings, our churches can offer a tremendous witness to those in need.

Setting up a team to coordinate emergency preparedness is vital—and something I'll discuss in chapter 8. The team will need time to plan relief efforts and to develop reserves of supplies. While everyone involved with the Y2K situation hopes the disruption is minimal or even nonexistent, good preparation could not only bring comfort to those in need, but the opportunity to present a gospel message of hope and salvation. If no major Y2K disruption happens in your community, the preparations you make need not go for naught: natural disasters and emergencies strike just about everywhere, sooner or later, so these preparations can have a dual purpose. Or, when a disaster strikes another part of the world, your church can have a hand in meeting those needs.

While it is possible that the Y2K situation could bring confusion and crisis, there are many who believe it might also sow the seeds of tremendous revival. Will your church be ready?

Y2K Solutions at Work

Just like the church, the place where you work has many dimensions, many facets. First and foremost, your place of business is just that—a business. It is there to provide a service and in turn earn money for the shareholders or owners. In so doing, a business will also provide goods or services to its customers, and jobs for its employees. Like a three-legged stool, a company needs management, workers, and customers in order to successfully stand up.

But for most of us, our jobs are a little bit more. They're a miniature community, sometimes even a "family," if you know what I mean. The people with whom we work aren't just mind-numbed robots who soullessly go about their daily tasks. Dedication to the job may be first and foremost; but it's also nice when an office or store or factory is collegial as well.

When you work in a place for a given amount of time, it's natural to form friendships and build relationships with your coworkers. Indeed, more than one study in recent years indicates that many of us find our marriage partners while on the job. (Sometimes, as a friend at AT&T once told me, we're too busy to socialize elsewhere!) Thus, our concerns about Y2K and the office will likely go a little beyond the simple question of whether or not our particular job will be secure.

It is conceivable that some businesses will no longer be in business after the Year 2000 bug hits. A business that is struggling or marginal could be put under by nonfunctioning systems, debtors who can't or won't pay, and problems with suppliers. Taking the approach that this is "someone else's problem" is one way to increase your company's chances of joining the ranks of those firms shuttered by a computer bug.

Irene Dec, Prudential Insurance Company of America's vice president in charge of Year 2000 programs, told the House of Representatives Ways and Means Committee last year of eight steps she suggests for each small business to effectively deal with the Y2K situation.[3] Let's look at those steps, which I'll annotate with some practical suggestions:

1. *Secure executive commitment:* If you are the owner or manager of a business, you have de-

cided to be informed about the Y2K problem; that's why you're reading this book. Share what you learn with your company's executives and get their commitment to help make sure your business is Y2K ready.

2. *Establish a Year 2000 program office:* If your company is large enough—and if it hasn't been done already—assemble a team to focus on the various facets of Y2K compliance: internal computer systems, external suppliers and business partners, utilities. Ideally, these should be people who are already dealing with these matters. Remember: you are a customer of the bank, telephone company, electric utility, computer manufacturer, etc.—demand the kind of service you give your customers.

3. *Identify critical applications:* It's not just all your PCs, peripherals, and desktop software that are critical to your business. It's operating systems, networking software, and the internal phone system (including voice mail). Also, how long could your business work effectively without a fax machine? Without an alarm system? Without electronically controlled locks on doors? Without elevators? Without heating or air conditioning? All these need to be verified, and that will likely include your landlord and other suppliers.

4. *Stop all other technological projects:* Dec, in her Congressional testimony said, "Place all other systems work on hold until your Year 2000 project is completed. At this point, there isn't time for anything else."[4] I would agree, as far as computer systems are concerned. Clearly, though, you cannot let your entire business fall apart over this

matter. Indeed, keeping your business up and running is the goal of all this Y2K planning!

5. *Devote time to testing:* He'd never say it publicly, but in private former Soviet leader Mikhail Gorbachev was said to cringe every time former President Reagan quoted "Dovai na provai," or "Trust, but verify," when talking about arms control. Tough darts, as they used to say, for Gorbachev, and tough darts for anyone in your office who groans about verifying whether or not your systems, when fixed, are Y2K compliant. Better to find out before January 1, 2000, than afterwards.

6. *Develop contingency plans:* This suggestion might rate a "Duh" from most of us, but it's still important. If you find that your business isn't going to make the deadline for Y2K in any area, or if you feel extra insurance would be in order, then move ahead with contingency plans.

7. *Review and assess business partner risks:* "No man is an island," poet John Donne wrote, and no business is either. If the people whom you count on for supplies and services aren't Y2K compliant, find out when they will be and determine what you will do for alternatives.

8. *Validate desktops:* Last, but not least, it's important to make sure that your desktop PCs are Y2K compliant. I've mentioned the Norton 2000 program from Symantec, and there are other good ways of checking your programs and data files, as well as your hardware. Testing should be done early and more than once.

As we saw with regard to personal finances in chapter 4, the prudent business or organization will want to make sure all its records are in order and that there are back-up copies of financial statements and the like, in order to make sure that the Year 2000 doesn't catch a firm unawares. Now may also be a good time to keep some traveler's checks or even cash on hand (secured, of course) in case there is a serious banking disruption. Prepaying some suppliers may also be a sound idea.

There's No Place like Home for Y2K Fixes

Although chapter 9 will take a more in-depth view of how families can prepare for potential Year 2000 disruptions, here are some initial thoughts on what to look for around the house:

1. *Household systems:* Heating, air conditioning, lawn sprinklers, security systems—all these should be checked and verified as being Y2K compliant. While many controllers for these systems may only rely on a 24-hour clock, some may have embedded chips that use year dates as well. Now is the time to review these and, if necessary, contemplate replacements. Examine the item for the date of manufacture and verify the company's Y2K compliance by calling the manufacturer or supplier.

2. *Verify utility services:* Electricity, water, gas, and telephone services are crucial in most homes. Be a dogged consumer and find out what your local suppliers are doing to prepare for Year 2000.

3. *Check consumer electronics:* If you depend on cable or satellite TV, a programmable VCR, or other devices, it might be wise to examine these for Y2K compliance. As mentioned elsewhere, not being

able to tape an episode of *Touched by an Angel* may be inconvenient, but having to replace these items after January 1 could be difficult if there are other breakdowns.

4. *Ask about insurance coverage:* Check with your agent to make sure your homeowner's or renter's policy will cover any damages due to Y2K failures. If not, see whether you can obtain separate damage/disaster insurance, just in case.

5. *Check your PCs:* The same advice given to those in business applies here. Check and verify your computers so that you don't lose valuable data files. (Of course, if your personal records are on a Macintosh rather than a PC, you have nothing to worry about.)

None of these are extremely complicated steps if you start early. And now that you know some things to do, it's time to get to work!

Endnotes

1. Since no printed book can give you fully up-to-date information, for the latest on Y2K you can visit this author's Website at www.kellner2000.com for links to the latest Y2K news and information. Unlike books, sites on the Internet can be updated constantly.

2. Text in this section is adapted from Mark A. Kellner, "The Bug Goes to Church," *Computing Today,* Jan./Feb. 1999: 14.

3. Irene Dec, Testimony, House Ways & Means Committee, Subcommittee on Oversight, 7 May 1998.

4. Ibid.

Chapter 8

Preparing to Minister and Witness

The King will reply, "I tell you the truth, whatever you did for one of the least of these brothers of mine, you did for me."

Matthew 25:40

Religion that God our Father accepts as pure and faultless is this: to look after orphans and widows in their distress.

James 1:27

By now it should be clear that the Year 2000 situation is one that has the potential to affect multiple millions of people in the United States and around the world. The only question is just how much of an effect there will be.

In this chapter, I will examine ways in which individuals, neighborhoods, communities, and congregations can take steps to be ready both to help those in need and to offer a message of faith to their neighbors who might be fearful during such a time. In chapter 1, I suggested this might be the greatest opportunity for Christian witness—in every sense—since the first Pentecost. You will remember from the book of Acts how the early church at Jerusalem helped those in need; the reminder from James cited above about what constitutes "pure" religion is a timely one in this context.

I will divide this chapter between ways to meet physical needs and those for meeting spiritual ones. The split between meeting physical needs and spiritual ones may seem a strange dichotomy to some. The American Red Cross doesn't spend its disaster relief efforts on preaching, and some ministers might feel happier leaving the task of meeting physical needs to someone else. But I am convinced, as was William Booth, the founder of The Salvation Army, that one cannot preach effectively to someone who is starving or homeless or cold. Thus, I would respectfully suggest that authentic religious witness would combine both facets.

Meeting Physical Needs

Two weeks after the 1995 Hanshin Earthquake in Kobe, Japan, I stood amidst the skeletal frames and debris of a downtown cluster of shops. In many of them, the people who ran the stores had dwelt in small rooms at the rear of the stores. This shopping area was old enough that the buildings either collapsed easily or caught fire easily. The results were tragic: hundreds of souls perished. Amid the wreckage were flowers and other memorials to the deceased. As I stood with a Salvation Army officer (an ordained minister) from Tokyo, he bowed his head and prayed, in a quiet voice, for those whose earthly lives were snuffed out in a matter of seconds.

A short distance away was a schoolyard that had become a refugee camp of sorts for those displaced by the trembler. The national defense forces had erected large bathing tents where people could wash up, men in one group, then women. The temporary dwellings erected by the people in the camp were not shabby in many cases, but neat and orderly, even a bit comfortable.

I'll never forget the reaction of most of these people when a Salvation Army delegation or other visitors would swing by. There was appreciation, yes, and the politeness for which the Japanese are renowned. But the face of each person would brighten, genuinely, when someone expressed an interest in his or her welfare, whether it was an Army officer or a well-known reporter from the NHK television network who was also on hand.

If the disruptions of any Year 2000 breakdowns approach the severity of an earthquake—and I pray they do not—there will be plenty of hurting people out there. In a severe disruption where emergency services are strained and where homes might be destroyed in fire or other circumstances, the need to comfort and protect those injured will be great.

So, too, will be the needs of the elderly and infirm who might face a week or two or longer without essential services or without benefit payments and other assistance. If the water isn't running or the electricity is down, if stores are not able to be restocked, there will be a great need among those who perhaps could not prepare in advance.

How can communities and churches prepare to help others? Some simple—and not so simple—steps suggest themselves. Here are seven steps to begin with:

1. *Begin with God's wisdom.* For any endeavor such as this to succeed, it is essential to seek the will

of God in every step of the process. Make this a time for joint Bible study and prayer, as well as for physical work. Pray for the people your group will be led to help; pray for each other in your group.

2. *Plan early.* Just as you will want to make your plans for individual Year 2000 preparations long *before* the dreaded day arrives, so, too, will you want to get together with neighbors or church members to plan activities related to this.

Appointing a committee and surveying the situation in your community will be extremely useful—as I've said elsewhere, December 15, 1999, is *not* the ideal time to start planning. As part of your planning, it's a good idea to cross-check your plans with local disaster relief officials and other agencies in your municipality. This will help you give to the *needy,* not the greedy, and will avoid duplication of services. If local agencies are already planning to be well stocked with food, for example, your church need not take that on. But perhaps there are other specific areas you could concentrate on, such as the medical needs of homebound individuals or transportation needs of families with young children.

3. *Let everyone have his or her say.* That's what Rev. Mitch Dennis, pastor of the Ely Gospel Tabernacle, in Ely, Minnesota, plans to do. The church, in the northern part of the state, is putting a premium on letting those in the congregation have their say about preparations so that all can agree. Dennis, a veteran church planter and former missionary, said his congregation has a committee dealing with various tactics for Year 2000 matters,

and the panel will propose solutions to the church board.

"I think it's just a matter of management and allowing people to express their excitement, not to let them go wild but allow them to have that expression," Dennis added.[1]

4. *Get basic information on distribution of services.* Whatever you want to do, first check with local agencies to see if someone else is already handling that area of need. If you believe that your community will need food supplies, then check for what distribution systems are already in place. If your group or church isn't already running a food bank or food pantry, contact a neighboring group that is so you can learn the best way to set one up for your area. If you don't have any such resources in your area, contact a national group such as Second Harvest[2] or a local agricultural extension office. If you are going to be helping out in some other area of need, for example, medical needs, first check to see what sorts of plans are already in place for this.

5. *Prioritize activities and schedule people.* Again, the time to start is early, before the time of need. Be sure there will be people available at that time to help. If your entire congregation is planning to steal away into the woods to await the new millennium, you may face a shortage of personnel.

6. *Keep enthusiasm high.* As the Year 2000 date approaches, changing developments may increase— or lessen—enthusiasm for this project on the part of people in your group. If they're ready to work hard, that's great; if encouragement is needed, remember that anything you can do to help those

117

in need in your community will be appreciated by those you help. Even if Y2K effects are mild to minor in your area, this new millennium will still be an opportunity to reflect God's love to others.

7. *Add a spiritual dimension.* Tell everyone you work with on the outside why you're involved in these plans. When you assist people, let them know what motivates this effort. And consider offering a small Gospel of John or similar literature along with each food parcel given to someone in need.

Working from such a standpoint will give your efforts even greater success. But I cannot emphasize enough the importance of making your plans as early—and as thoroughly—as possible. In the aftermath of a severe Y2K disaster, should one occur, communications and co-ordination among groups would be exponentially more difficult.

In discussing the theme of this chapter with a newsman at a Christian radio station, he raised a good point: "You're saying churches should disrupt their main work—or add to it—and stockpile all this food for something which even you admit may not happen."

He's correct, of course, on both counts. I'm suggesting that churches and community groups take on extra work and perhaps delay some projects in order to prepare for something that may not take place. What's the answer for this? In my view, it's not a bad idea for Christians—and other good-hearted people in any community—to exercise as much concern and compassion for those in need as they can.

A parable Jesus told in Matthew 25 concludes with a

stern assessment: "whatever you did for one of the least of these brothers of mine, you did for me" (Matthew 25:40). While the debate between thinkers such as Ronald Sider (*Rich Christians in an Age of Hunger*) and his critics is beyond the scope of this volume, I believe that reasonable people on both sides of the debate can agree that we should—we must—do as much for our neighbors as we can. That said, I wonder if the Year 2000 situation might not spur many of us towards greater efforts in fulfillment of Jesus' injunction to help "the least of these."

Offering a Spiritual Witness

One of the things I saw in Kobe, Japan—and in the San Fernando Valley of Los Angeles the year before when a massive earthquake hit there—is that people who have endured a major disruption or disaster need reassurance. They need hope and an assurance of the future. They need the very things that Christians have in abundance, or at least they should.

Sharing with people during such turbulent times may seem difficult, but it has been observed that it is just at those trying times when people need to be confronted with the good news of hope in Jesus. If you don't believe me, listen to Dr. George H. Gallup, the premiere pollster in the United States, who in recent years has studied trends involving churches. Recently, he spoke with *The Washington Times* about the trends in Washington State, which ranks lowest for church attendance. Washington, with its boom economy, is a place where life for many is good. Those who are satisfied with their lives, he said, aren't usually ripe for conversion: "Life is good and challenging for them. Their health is vibrant, and they don't see any need for God. Most people come to a stronger belief in God after going through valleys."[3]

What was said about these Washingtonians, I believe, applies to the rest of the country, if not the world. Those who do not sense a need in their lives may rapidly change their minds if confronted with breakdowns. The time to offer hope is when a valley experience confronts those who are victimized by Year 2000 disruptions.

One of my favorite sermons was preached by Tony Campolo, and it covers the resurrection of Jesus Christ—as seen from the vantage point of the Crucifixion. "It's Friday," Campolo says, talking about the traditional day known as Good Friday, *"but Sunday's coming!"*—the morning after the Resurrection. Things are bad, but with God and Jesus, they can improve.

Couple that thought with the words expressed in Jeremiah 29:11 (NASB): "'For I know the plans that I have for you,' declares the Lord, 'plans for welfare and not for calamity to give you a future and a hope.'" This good news takes on an even better meaning when you consider the Hebrew words in back of them. That first instance of *plans,* for example, is in the active tense—the implication is that God is planning these good things right now. Also, *a future and a hope* is more properly rendered as "an expected end." Just as when you board a train for Boston you can expect, reasonably, to get there, God's plan for those who trust him through Jesus is a soft landing at the end of your journey.

When dealing with people who have undergone crisis, it might be better to approach them from this standpoint than from the more traditional route of taking the largest Thompson Chain Reference Bible you can find, planting it under the sinner's nose, and ranting at him or her about hell and damnation.

Not everyone will be willing to hear what you have to say, even at a time of extreme crisis. But some will hear, and some will respond. The challenge will be to allow God to work through us to reach those who will be made willing through these circumstances.

There are many preparations that can be made for such efforts, and plenty of books and training materials for personal evangelism.[4] Evangelism resources are likely to be available within your denomination, and of course through local Christian bookstores. But, as with the preparation for ministry to meet physical needs, the most important step any group can take is to pray and seek God's will on this matter. Preparation and prayer are the keys to success in meeting human need, both in terms of temporal needs and eternal ones.

Endnotes

1. Mitch Dennis, quoted in Kellner, "Y2K: A Secular Apocalypse?" *Christianity Today*, 11 Jan. 1999: 54.

2. For those who are not familiar with the Chicago-based charity, Second Harvest is the country's sixth largest charity, according to the Chronicle of Philanthropy. It has a national network of 188 regional food banks serving all 50 states and Puerto Rico. The group distributes one billion pounds of donated food and grocery product annually, reaching 26 million hungry Americans—almost one of every 10 people in the country. The network supports nearly 50,000 local charitable agencies, operating more than 94,000 food programs. (Second Harvest news release, 18 Dec. 1998). You can contact them at 312-263-2303 or www.secondharvest.org.

3. Quoted in Julia Duin, "Gallup Poll Finds Washington State Least Churchgoing," *The Washington Times* (6 Jan. 1999): A2.

4. Perhaps the best known evangelism tool is the presentation of the "Four Spiritual Laws" developed by Bill Bright, founder of the Campus Crusade for Christ. That group offers materials that can be used in presenting these laws to people. Campus Crusade for Christ can be found online (www.campuscrusade.org/index.htm).

Chapter 9

Planning for the Home

At that time the kingdom of heaven will be like ten virgins who took their lamps and went out to meet the bridegroom. Five of them were foolish and five were wise. The foolish ones took their lamps but did not take any oil with them. The wise, however, took oil in jars along with their lamps.

Jesus of Nazareth, Matthew 25:1-4

Preparedness is everyone's job. Not just government agencies but all sectors of society—service providers, businesses, civic and volunteer groups, industry associations and neighborhood associations, as well as *every individual citizen*—should plan ahead for disaster. During the first few hours or days following a disaster, essential services may not be available. *People must be ready to act on their own.*

Federal Emergency Management Administration (emphasis added)

Theologians might object—just a bit—to my using a parable about the kingdom of heaven to illustrate the need for preparedness in the face of an emergency.

Jesus' return, most agree, will be anything but an emergency situation—it will be the *end* of emergencies, and for all time!

However, the concept of being foolish or wise—unprepared or ready—is, I believe, extremely valid to our discussion here. And no less an authority (when it comes to disasters, that is) than the federal agency responsible for disaster relief agrees. According to the Federal Emergency Management Administration, we *must* be ready to cope with disaster.

Self-reliance is a concept at the bedrock of American life, but frankly it's one many of us have "gone soft" on in recent years. For many of us, it's understandable. Life has, in general, been good and free of disruption for most of the United States, for most of the past thirty or forty years. Yes, we've had periodic earthquakes, and yes, the 1970s saw two energy crises that prompted long lines at gas pumps, but for most of us we've had few complaints.

Thus, when disaster strikes, our "softness" shows: Following the 1992 impact of Hurricane Andrew in Florida, one person laid the responsibility for meeting daily needs at an unusual door: "Where's President Bush?" this person asked a television reporter. "There are people starving down here!"

You might disagree with me, but I'll tell you—I'm not depending on the President of the United States, the Vice President, the Speaker of the House, or the Governor of California for my daily meals. If an earthquake struck tomorrow, I would not expect them to show up at my door with a hot lunch.

The smart answer, then, is to prepare for disasters as best as possible. Otherwise, you may be at the mercy of relief operations that will be under siege from other folks who haven't prepared. The Year 2000 crisis isn't the only potential disaster any of us will face. Earthquakes, hurricanes, tornadoes, fires, and floods—any of these can strike, usually without warning. While some disasters are less likely than others, it is probable that many of us will confront a minor or major disruption at some time in the future. That's why it makes sense to prepare for a potential disaster whether or not the Year 2000 bug causes a major disruption. As I've already said in several radio interviews—better to have the supplies and not need them, than to need them and not have them!

In that spirit, here are suggestions on what to prepare and how, taken from the Federal Emergency Management Administration.[1]

Water, the First Necessity

You can go for several days without food (for me, it might even be longer, but that's another story). But you can't go for long without clean, safe water to drink.

FEMA recommends storing at least a two-week supply of water for each family member. How much a person will need would vary by age, physical condition, activity, diet, and climate. A normally active person needs to drink at least two quarts of water each day. Hot environments can double that amount. (Children, nursing mothers, and those who are ill will need more.)

The best storage containers for water are plastic soft drink bottles that have been cleaned and rinsed. Food-grade plastic buckets and drums can also be used, FEMA says, as can enamel-lined metal containers.

Before storing water, guard against the growth of

125

microorganisms by treating the water with chlorine bleach. FEMA suggests the use of liquid bleach containing 5.25 percent sodium hypochlorite and no soap. Add four drops of bleach per quart of water, or two "scant" teaspoons per ten gallons, and stir. After mixing, seal the containers tightly and store in a secure, dry place.

FEMA has some other unique suggestions about water sources inside and outside the home. You can drain the water that is standing in pipes and even the water in your waterbed. In the latter case, however, your best bet is to drain and fill the waterbed annually, and refill it with fresh water containing two ounces of bleach per 120 gallons. (First check your waterbed manual to see if the addition of bleach would harm the plastic liner, of course.)

Outdoor water sources such as rainwater, streams, rivers, ponds, and lakes can be used, FEMA advises, but only if the water has been purified. Boiling water (a rolling boil for ten minutes, then letting the water cool before drinking); chlorination (with bleach); and purification tablets (available at camping, surplus, and some drug stores) are the best ways of doing this.

In terms of advance preparation, it is also a good idea to buy and keep bottled water around the house. Many communities have warehouse clubs and other "superstores" where bargains on such water can be found. Stockpiling a few cases of water might not be a bad idea.

How Much Food Do You Need?

The answer to how much food you need may surprise you. According to FEMA:

If activity is reduced, healthy people can survive on half their usual food intake for an extended period and without any food for many days. Food, unlike water, may be rationed safely, except for children and pregnant women.

If your water supply is limited, try to avoid foods that are high in fat and protein, and don't stock salty foods, since they will make you thirsty. Try to eat salt-free crackers, whole grain cereals and canned foods with high liquid content.[2]

While you will doubtless see advertisements for prepackaged "survival" foods, FEMA advises that such purchases are not necessary for a short-term food supply. Canned and boxed foods are easier to manage and use, and are more familiar, which can be a comfort in trying times.

FEMA advises keeping a two-week supply of food on hand, which can be accomplished by just buying a little extra on a regular basis and then storing these properly.

Canned foods should be kept in a dry place where the temperature is fairly cool—not above seventy degrees Fahrenheit but not below freezing. To protect boxed foods from pests and extend their shelf life, store the boxes in tightly closed plastic bins or metal containers. The key is to make sure the containers can be as tightly closed as possible, to keep out pests.

Don't forget to rotate the emergency food supply. Use foods before they go bad, and replace them with fresh supplies dated with a permanent marker. To ensure proper rotation, place new items at the back of the storage area and older ones in front. Also, you should inspect your reserves periodically to make sure there are no broken seals or dented containers.[3]

Important Nutrition Tips

FEMA advises that in a crisis we focus on maintaining strength. The agency offers this advice[4]:

- Eat at least one well-balanced meal each day.
- Drink enough liquid to enable your body to function properly (two quarts a day).
- Take in enough calories to enable you to do any necessary work.
- Include vitamin, mineral, and protein supplements in your stockpile to ensure adequate nutrition.

An Overall Family Plan

One of the purposes of this book is to provide authoritative, accurate information. In that spirit, we reprint below portions of a FEMA document called "Your Family Disaster Plan."[5] The advice here is more succinct and useful than anything else I have seen. "Families can and do cope with disaster by preparing in advance and working together as a team," FEMA advises. Follow the steps listed here to create your family's disaster plan. Knowing what to do is your best protection, and it is your responsibility.

4 Steps to Safety[6]

1. *Find Out What Could Happen to You*
   - Contact your local Red Cross chapter or emergency management office—be prepared to take notes.
   - Ask about animal care after a disaster. Animals are not allowed inside emergency shelters because of health regulations.

- Find out how to help elderly or disabled persons, if needed.
- Find out about the disaster plans at your workplace, your children's school or day-care center, and other places where your family spends time.

2. *Create a Disaster Plan*
   - Meet with your family and discuss why you need to prepare for unexpected events. Explain the dangers matter-of-factly to children. Plan to share responsibilities and work together as a team.
   - Discuss the types of crises that are most likely to happen. Explain what to do in each case.
   - Discuss what to do in an evacuation. Plan how to take care of your pets.

3. *Complete This Checklist*
   If you haven't already done so, instruct your family in basic emergency response.
   - Post emergency telephone numbers by phones (fire, police, ambulance, etc.).
   - Teach children how and when to call 9-1-1 or your local Emergency Medical Services number for emergency help.
   - Show each family member how and when to turn off the water, gas, and electricity at the main switches.
   - Check to see that you have adequate insurance coverage.
   - Stock emergency supplies and assemble a Disaster Supplies Kit.
   - Take a Red Cross first aid and CPR class.

4. *Practice and Maintain Your Plan*

- Replace stored water and food at regular intervals.
- Test and recharge your fire extinguisher(s) according to manufacturer's instructions.

Neighbors Helping Neighbors

Working with neighbors can save lives and property. Meet with your neighbors to plan how the neighborhood could work together if needed, until help arrives. If you're a member of a neighborhood organization, such as a home association or crime watch group, introduce disaster preparedness as a new activity. Know your neighbors' special skills (e.g., medical, technical) and consider how you could help neighbors who have special needs, such as disabled and elderly persons. Make plans for child care in case parents can't get home.

Emergency Supplies

Keep enough supplies in your home to meet your needs for at least three days. Assemble a *Disaster Supplies Kit* with items you may need in an evacuation. Store these supplies in sturdy, easy-to-carry containers such as backpacks, duffle bags, or covered trash containers. Include:

- A three-day supply of water (one gallon per person per day) and food that won't spoil.
- One change of clothing and footwear per person, and one blanket or sleeping bag per person.
- A first aid kit that includes your family's prescription medications.
- Emergency tools including a battery-powered radio, flashlight, and plenty of extra batteries.
- An extra set of car keys and cash.

- Sanitation supplies.
- Special items for infant, elderly, or disabled family members.
- An extra pair of glasses.
- Keep important family documents in a waterproof container. Keep a smaller kit in the trunk of your car.

Utilities

- Locate the main electrical box, water service main, and natural gas main. Learn how and why to turn these utilities off. Teach all responsible family members. Keep necessary tools near gas and water shut-off valves.
- Remember, turn off the utilities only if you suspect the lines are damaged or if you are instructed to do so. If you turn the gas off, you will need a professional to turn it back on.

Preparing yourself and your family for these eventualities is a sensible move, no matter what happens on January 1, 2000. In addition to the advice given above, I would add some minor and major suggestions:

1. Get major (and regular) dental and medical work taken care of in advance of the end of 1999.
2. If you are taking prescription medication, make sure you have an adequate supply (at least a month extra).
3. Along with battery-operated radios, there are several models of hand-powered radios you might want to purchase.
4. Having emergency cleaning items, such as moist towelettes and "waterless" soap (antibacterial) is also a good idea.

5. Take care of pet needs. Several of the suggestions above from FEMA involve protecting pets, and I would be remiss in closing this chapter without adding a word on behalf of the companion animals that share many of our homes. Clearly, making sure their veterinary needs are taken care of before the end of 1999 is important, as is maintaining adequate supplies of the food those animals need. The reason for doing this is not just because the animals depend on us for their well-being. The other is that during a time of frustration or uncertainty, having a friendly dog or cat around can ease stress. In the temporary dwellings of Kobe, my heart melted a bit when I saw one family grooming and caring for a cat who obviously was dear to them.

I also side with Catherine Booth, cofounder of The Salvation Army who was such a strong advocate of animal rights that she had written into the original covenant signed by members of that church a promise that they would properly care for (and never abuse) any animal that came into that person's care. I don't worship my pets, but I believe that just as God expects me to be good to the people I meet, he wants me to do well by our animal friends.

Endnotes

1. FEMA, "Preparedness," online (www.fema.gov/pte/pre1.htm).

2. Publications at FEMA Library, online (www.fema.gov/library/lib07.htm).

3. FEMA, "Emergency Food and Water Supplies," 1192, rev. 1998 (www.fema.gov/pte/foodwtr.htm).

4. "Emergency Food and Water Supplies."

5. FEMA, "Your Family Disaster Plan," online (www.fema.gov/pte/displan.htm).

6. "Your Family Disaster Plan."

Chapter 10

Helping Children and the Elderly

Children, obey your parents in the Lord, for this is right. "Honor your father and mother"—which is the first commandment with a promise—"that it may go well with you and that you may enjoy long life on the earth." Fathers, do not exasperate your children; instead, bring them up in the training and instruction of the Lord.

Paul of Tarsus, Ephesians 6:1-4

One of the reasons this book was written was to offer sound, sensible, and practical advice on coping with whatever the Year 2000 brings our way. Clearly, one element of that will be in our family life, helping children and the elderly in our homes through a potentially difficult time.

As has been stated several times in these pages, no one can say with any certainty at this moment just what, exactly, will transpire when the clock strikes midnight on December 31, 1999. While I suspect, and pray, that any disruptions will be negligible, the prudent view of the circumstances and potential effects—at this writing—require the conclusion that things may not flow as smoothly as desired.

That being the case, it would also seem prudent to consider the effects a major disruption could have on children and the elderly. What follows is some common sense advice, not medical or psychological counseling. For individuals with special emotional or physical needs, a consultation with a qualified professional would be in order.

Point One: Your Family Should Be a Center of Calm

However challenging a set of circumstances may be, it is in the family where we should be able to find refuge and security in the midst of crisis. Few of us are flawless in executing such a belief, but we can all try to do better—and this new situation may be the catalyst some of us need.

Clearly the way for families to center themselves in the middle of strife is to have a solid dependence on God, and a relationship with him through Jesus Christ is what the Bible offers as the way to peace with God.

With a spiritual routine established, you can move on to the next step, sound preparations for emergency and disaster. The key steps in this were covered in chapter 9, and as your family participates in getting ready for what *may* transpire, they will have assurance that you are all prepared.

Along the way, be sure to have fun. Take time to be with and share with your family members, and try to live in what Dale Carnegie once called "day-tight" compartments. When you think about it, all we really have is the present day, the current moment, so it makes sense to live within this time and not worry (too much) about tomorrow.

Point Two: This Doesn't Have to Scare Children

As 1999 progresses, it is highly likely that many of us will see and hear dire predictions sure to strike fear in most hearts. When dealing with children, however, there are ways to minimize the natural (and perhaps unusual) fears that might arise.

First, involve the kids—in some fashion—in your preparations. Let them see that what you are doing isn't scary, per se, but rather something prudent that a family should do to prepare for any sort of emergency or short-term crisis. Let everyone help, and let everyone share in the workload.

Obviously, there are things you would want an older child to handle that you would not dream of letting a toddler tackle. But just about everyone can do something to help prepare for Y2K, and in so doing, everyone can get a feeling of calm and readiness.

It also makes sense to sit down with the children and calmly inform them that things may be a little difficult around the New Year. Again, there's no reason to scare the socks off anyone, but saying that there might be some problems, and explaining why, can calm fears and build faith. Indeed, letting everyone know that you are aware of the situation and are working to prepare should lessen everyone's fears.

Point Three: Some of This Can Be Fun

It won't be a picnic if the power is off for several weeks, but positioning a Y2K situation as just a really long camping exercise might put kids in a good frame of mind. Between now and the end of 1999, it might be useful to go on a camping trip and practice some skills, such as cooking, cleaning, setting up camp and the like—besides, it's a great way to promote family togetherness.

Making every aspect of your Year 2000 preparations a game might take a little extra effort, but it should pay dividends in keeping the stress level down. Canning food, storing supplies, getting everything in order may well go better with a metaphorical "spoonful of sugar," as Mary Poppins would have said.

This is another good reason, in my view, to begin any Year 2000 preparations early. Should you wake up on December 20, 1999, and decide to start planning, you will probably be more rushed than otherwise, and those around you will notice the tension that results. Take it slow and easy, and you'll be more likely to convey an attitude of calm.

How you arrange all this will be determined in large measure by the ages and talents of your kids and by the capabilities of any older persons in your home. But starting early, involving everyone, and making this all fun, are good keys to coping.

Point Four: Parents, Grandparents, or In-laws May Need Special Assurance

If you have some senior citizens nearby—your parents

or your in-laws or a grandparent or two—they may need special attention and consideration. Be sure to sit down and talk with them about any concerns they may have, and as part of your emergency planning, be sure to stock up on any medicines or supplies they might need.

When I walked through the streets of Kobe after their 1995 earthquake, I was told that one reason for a high casualty rate among older people there was that the elders would often live on the first floor of a house, and when the quake hit, the heavy tile roofs collapsed, trapping the occupants below. The likelihood of earthquakes hitting because of Y2K is virtually nil, but the example does make me believe it is wise to include the needs of all those in your household when making plans.

Point Five: God Is in Control

At the end of this chapter—and the end of this book—it is wise for us all to realize one thing: that God is in control of all aspects of our lives, and that he wants good for us. Conveying that message to your family, to your friends and colleagues, should offer some hope while you are planning to cope with what comes.

Stay informed, yes. Prepare for some disruption, yes. Make sure things are in order, of course. But ultimately, our security must rest in God. Living or dying, well or ill, in affluence or more modest means, our only true hope is in the Lord, who created all things and sustains them.

Recognizing this, storing it in our hearts, is perhaps the best basic preparation we can make.

Chapter 11

As This Book Goes to Press . . .

Massive power failures. Societal collapse. Riots in the streets. Citizens urged to take up guns in defense of their homes and freeze-dried meals. Are these the images you think of when considering the arrival of the Year 2000 and what may happen to computers on that date?

If you do, you're not alone. The first part of 1999 is seeing near panic sweeping parts of the country, largely centered on Y2K. *Time* magazine, a journal not usually given to wild speculation, had an "end of the world" cover on its January 18, 1999, issue. There's a countdown to the millennium clock sitting on my desk, a Christmas gift from my mother-in-law, ticking away the days, hours, minutes, and seconds until January 1 of next year. And on Christian and secular radio stations, there's an increasing number of ads for prepackaged diets and wood-burning stoves, "available in six to ten weeks." Just give your credit card number.

Lehman's hardware in Kidron, Ohio, has been overrun. This firm specializes in gasoline-powered refrigerators and wood-burning stoves, sold mostly to their Amish neighbors who shun electricity and to missionaries headed to places without electric power. Already some key items are out-of-stock until the middle of 2000. The ever-so-sad part of all this is that while the Lehman firm's business is doubling this year, they have had to say no to some families headed for the mission field who would need a wood-burning stove regardless of Y2K. The survivalist-oriented customers got there first.[1]

It's a frightening time, and as you have read this book, you may see some things to be concerned about. *However*, it must be noted that right now, today, in the early weeks of 1999, there's good news to report about the world's progress in gearing up for the Year 2000. It may not be pain free, but it's very likely that things *will not* be as bad as some originally thought.

There's Good News Tonight!

Back in the 1930s, one of the pioneer radio broadcasters was a fellow named Gabriel Heatter whose trademark saying was, "Good evening, ladies and gentlemen, THERE'S GOOD NEWS TONIGHT." As this book is being readied for printing, I'm happy to report some good news concerning the Year 2000.

The good news is that apparently great progress is being made on the Y2K situation, so much so that we may not be in as desperate a shape as some previously believed.

I have been loathe to take on, specifically, the claims of some in the community that the Year 2000 bug is going to lead to The End of the World As We Know It (or TEOTWAWKI, as you'll see it on the Internet) because—and it bears repeating—even at this writing no one can say with absolute certainty what will or will not happen on January 1.

That said, however, the most recent reports indicate better news about the Y2K situation than you may have heard. In the face of the near panic we're seeing on the Y2K front, it is time for voices of calm to be heard. *The Wall Street Journal,* a media voice often noted for balance and even conservatism, featured the Reverend Steve Hewitt of Raymore, Missouri, on its front page. Steve is the founder and editor of *Christian Computing Magazine,* which generally reviews Bible study and church administration software packages. He's a solid, sincere believer, and he is someone who became alarmed at the mad dash many Christians have made towards survivalist instincts in relation to the Year 2000.

While many of us have heard all sorts of wild-eyed speculation about the Y2K situation, Steve Hewitt is among those debunking the craziest notions—the idea that American society will collapse for months and there will be massive chaos. Instead, he suggests, we need to verify the information we consider and weigh matters carefully.

He's right, and his correct view of this is one reason (but not the only one) for the number of footnotes in this book. Every major claim in these pages is documented. You can look up the sources of the information cited and see it yourself.

Part of Steve Hewitt's concern is that Christians could end up the laughing stocks of a nonbelieving world. I agree: If the Y2K "Ark" we are building is too elaborate, and unneeded, we won't be seen as loving people concerned for our neighbors but fringe-group wackos who are tossed with every wind of apocalyptic "doctrine" that comes from this week's seller of gold, grain grinders, or guns.

Along with verifying the information you read and

hear, I sincerely believe there needs to be *balance* in considering the Y2K situation. You will have read, in the latter chapters of this book, that experts suggest prudent safeguards of your financial records, and that the U.S. government recommends, for every family, a two-week emergency supply of food and water, as a matter of course. But that is far different from filling the basement with military-surplus food packs or trying to fit a wood-burning stove in your mid-city apartment. (And, please, don't try *that* unless you can vent the stove through a chimney!)

What Experts Now Say

Listen to the experts on the Y2K situation, and you'll hear encouraging words about Y2K. According to Lou Marcoccio, a research director at Gartner Group, a leading information technology research firm, there's encouragement in the area of embedded systems:

> The key issues concerning embedded chip failures are [one,] very few will fail, and [two,] of those that fail, the majority will fail right at the millennium, and the majority of these will only fail once—if they are active when the clock ticks over.

Marcoccio also says that Gartner Group has revised its estimates on which countries are most likely to have "mission critical failures" of the systems essential to daily life and commerce. Among the least likely, with a 15 percent risk, are the United States, Canada, Britain, Sweden, and Australia. Next, at a 33 percent risk, are nations such as Brazil, France, Italy, Mexico, and South Korea.

Germany, Saudi Arabia, Argentina, Japan, and Egypt

are among the countries facing a 50 percent risk, according to Gartner Group. Those most likely to have failures, a 66 percent chance, include China, Kenya, and Russia.[2]

Though the numbers could be more encouraging—after all, China is a nation of 1 billion people, while Russia and the former Soviet states total some 290 million people—it's not as bad as the declarations of some that the entire world will "shut down," lock, stock, and barrel.

Gartner is forecasting a wave of Y2K-related problems, beginning at various points through this year and stretching into the Year 2000 and a little beyond. If such a scenario plays out, many of us who study the situation hope the disruptions can be managed smoothly, at least in the United States.

Most overseas nations, clearly, face greater problems, and Marcoccio predicts some potential impact on the world economy during the first few years of the next decade. But again, response and reaction is key to minimizing the impact.

Recent reports indicate Russia and China are both mobilizing to tackle Y2K issues. For example, Russian officials told the Associated Press in February, 1999, that it would cost that nation some $3 billion (U.S.) to become Y2K compliant, money which may be difficult to find in a nation strapped for cash and investment capital.[3] In China, remediation cost estimates are lower—another $600 million is needed according to a report in the Beijing *Morning Post* picked up by the Associated Press.[4] China is not optimistic in every area: Beyond crucial systems for energy, transportation, communications, and defense, the government is providing little assistance, the report indicated.

Such dire news was countered, however, on February 2, 1999, at the World Economic Forum meeting in Davos, Switzerland. There, executives from many leading companies spoke and, according to a Reuters News Service report, said that Y2K disruptions in the industrialized world should be scattered and relatively minor.[5]

"The worst problem I see is the uncertainty when approaching that very day" before 2000 when clocks tick over, Goran Lindahl, chief executive officer of Swedish engineering and construction firm ABB Asea Brown Boveri. World readiness "varies widely. I do not forecast a lot of cataclysmic events, but I think there will be a lot of small things that will go wrong related to basically not having gotten totally prepared for the year 2K," Lindahl said.

According to Toshiba Corporation president Taizo Nichimuro, who also advises Japan's government on Y2K, that country is catching up: "Japan was a little bit late . . . but we are coming very close to the level of the United States or Europe."[6]

Good news, too, is coming on the airline front: According to *Travel Weekly,* the leading travel-trade industry publication, the airline industry is working intensively in its search for safety. "Corruption of an internal [reservation] system does not mean, however, that safety systems are in jeopardy—a fact that should allay the fears of travelers who believe planes will fall out of the sky next New Year's Eve," the magazine said in a news release.

According to Michele McDonald, aviation editor for the magazine, "the International Air Transport Association (IATA) is stressing that even in the least prepared situation, the issue is not safety. All safety systems have manual back-up systems that can be activated."

McDonald notes that the airlines, the Air Transport Association, the International Air Transport Association and airline suppliers are all collaborating and sharing information on common issues to ensure "no stone—or computer chip—is left unturned."[7]

As this year of 1999 advances, it is highly likely that we will see more progress reports that are optimistic, as well as a few that are pessimistic. The question is, which ones should you believe?

This is where something a pastor friend of mine called "sanctified common sense" comes in. As mentioned elsewhere in this book, it is wise for you to be prepared with information and knowledge. You should watch the newspapers and broadcast media to see what's happening in your community. The Christian Broadcasting Network (www.cbn.org) has an excellent Y2K Website chock full of all sorts of information; the same can be said for technology publishing giant Ziff-Davis (www.zdnet. com/zdy2k/), which is running a Y2K Website renowned for accuracy and balance. Other online sources of Y2K news are listed in the appendix of this book.

As you get news about Y2K from these and other sources, here's where the common sense comes in: Do not abandon common sense when reading or hearing about possible scenarios. Throughout this book, I have suggested things that *might* or *could* happen—I have purposely avoided saying they *will.* That's common sense, in my view: Even though I know a fair amount about technology, I know that I'm not omniscient!

At the moment, I am guardedly optimistic about what will happen at the beginning of next year. That could change to boisterous optimism, or it could regress to serious pessimism. What will influence my outlook is what I see happening in the days and weeks and months ahead. For example, I reside in Los Angeles. By June 30, 1999, the Department of Water and Power, a city agency, is supposed to be Y2K compliant. If they are—and that's verified—I'll feel a lot better about things than if I hear otherwise.

So it will go with other services and businesses with which I interact. And so it will probably go for you. But this is where your influence counts, as mentioned in other chapters. You have to make your views known to others, and you need to lobby those who provide essential services for the right answers.

Be observant and vigilant, and watch what happens. You may be pleasantly surprised at the outcome. And by the way, if none of our worst fears are realized, there are at least two benefits of the whole Y2K enterprise. One is that you will be more aware of how interconnected modern life is, and hopefully be a better, more informed consumer going forward. The second is that even the minimal preparations suggested in this book are prudent ones recommended for *any* family in *any* part of the country. Get ready and you're getting some extra insurance against a natural disaster as well.

Most important, though, I hope the run-up to January 1, 2000, will give Christians pause to think about what is happening in this world, and what their role should be. There are, I would suggest, some positive, spiritual benefits associated with Y2K.

The Spiritual Benefits of Y2K

It seems fitting to conclude this chapter and this entire book with a re-emphasis of the spiritual gains that Christians can have from Y2K.

This is the start of a new millennium. There will be

myriad opportunities to celebrate our faith in Christ, and to share that faith with our neighbors and coworkers. Some of that sharing may come through disaster relief; most will happen through personal evangelism.

In the U.S. and other Western societies, people often look at the start of a new calendar year as an opportunity to go out and start fresh. New Year's resolutions are popular, even if most are abandoned within the first thirty days of that year.

But if a simple New Year brings to mind a new beginning, think of what prospect a new millennium offers! This may be one of the greatest moments in which we can offer to nonbelievers the message that a true "clean slate" can be found in accepting Jesus Christ as Savior and Lord, and living a life with him at its center.

If there is one thing I have seen over the years, starting in 1972 when I wrote for a weekly newspaper in New York City, it's that people need, and want, hope. They want to know that something better can be theirs. They want to know that Someone cares about them, their needs, their future.

To a believer, such yearnings should come as no surprise. The answer—that such can be met in Christ—is a powerful and hopeful message that you and I can present to people as the days pass.

If believers, if people of faith, use the period before January 1, 2000, to prepare spiritually as well as physically, then the new millennium will dawn in better shape, regardless of what happens with some computer chips. If we share the gospel message of hope with those who are hurting and searching, then we will go a long way toward making that new millennium one of peace and joy.

Nothing is guaranteed in this life. We should each live

daily as if Christ might return at any moment. We can have the greatest success, however, if we use our time and our talents wisely to offer good news to those who are looking for some. That good news is Jesus Christ and what he offers. The messengers can be you and me.

It's time to get busy with these millennium preparations, wouldn't you agree? God bless you today.

Endnotes

1. Jay Lehman, telephone interview, 20 Jan. 1999.

2. Gartner Group, "Year 2000 Global State of Readiness and Risks to the General Business Community," Congressional testimony of Lou Marcoccio, 7 Oct. 1998 (www.gartner.com/public/static/aboutgg/pressrel/testimony1098.html).

3. Angela Charlton, "Russia Needs $3B To Fight Y2K Bug," Associated Press dispatch, 3 Feb. 1999.

4. "China Far From Solving Y2K Bug," Associated Press dispatch, 3 Feb. 1999.

5. Cited in Alice Ratcliffe, "Millennium Bug May Not Have A Nasty Bite," Reuters News Service, 2 Feb. 1999.

6. Ratcliffe.

7. *Travel Weekly* news release, "Airline Industry Will Soon Find Out Whether It Has Conquered the Millennium Bug, Reports Travel Weekly," 28 Jan. 1999.

Glossary

Computers and the Y2K situation have a particular terminology all their own. Here's a glossary of some of the terms you may encounter.

address An electronic mail address is the string of characters that you must give an electronic mail program to direct a message to a particular person. See also Internet address.

Altair The Altair was a pioneering microcomputer for which two young entrepreneurs, Bill Gates and Paul Allen, helped develop a programming language, launching a company known today as Microsoft Corp.

ASCII American Standard Code for Information Interchange. Text formatted in ASCII is "plain" text that can be read by or on almost any computer with virtually any word processor or text editor.

bit Binary digit: The smallest amount of information that may be stored in a computer.

bps Bits per second: A measure of data transmission speed.

byte One character of information, usually eight bits wide.

dedicated line A permanently connected private telephone line between two locations.

download To transfer files from one computer to another.

e-mail The vernacular abbreviation for electronic mail.

FAQ Frequently Asked Questions: A list of common questions with their answers. Most mailing lists and all network newsgroups provide FAQ postings on a regular basis. FAQ is a term now applied to lists of basic questions and answers about many subjects including Y2K.

Flame An Internet posting, usually on a newsgroup or via e-mail, that offers a negative, sometimes profane, response to another posting. You may receive flames in your Internet activity, but it is wise not to respond.

FTP File Transfer Protocol: The Internet standard high-level protocol for transferring files from one computer to another.

GB Gigabyte: A unit of data storage size that represents one billion characters of information.

Gb Gigabit: One billion bits of information (usually used to express a data transfer rate, as in 1 gigabit/second = lGbps).

Internet The global collection of interconnected regional and wide-area networks that use Internet Protocol as the network layer protocol.

Internet address An assigned number that identifies a host on an internet. It has two or three parts: network number, optional subnet number, and host number.

IP Internet Protocol: The means of communication for the Internet.

KB Kilobyte: A unit of data storage size that represents 1,024 characters of information.

Kb Kilobit: 1,024 bits of information (usually used to express a data transfer rate, as in 1 kilobit/second = 1Kbps).

LAN Local area network: A network that takes advantage of the proximity of computers to offer relatively efficient, higher speed communications than long-haul or wide-area networks.

MB Megabyte: A unit of data storage size that represents one million characters of information.

Mb Megabit: One million bits of information (usually used to express a data transfer rate, as in 1 megabit/second = 1Mbps).

Mainframe A large computer system designed for corporate computing.

Minicomputer A computer that functions as a multiuser system for up to several hundred users. Digital Equipment Corp. was the first to launch a minicomputer in 1959 with its PDP-1 for $20,000, an unheard-of low price for a computer in those days.

Microcomputer A computing device built around a microprocessor chip, such as the Intel Pentium II or PowerPC G3 chip. Generally called "personal" computers, microcomputers have proliferated during the last twenty years.

modem A piece of equipment that connects a computer to a data transmission line (typically a telephone line).

PPP Point-to-Point Protocol: provides a method for transmitting datagrams over serial point-to-point links.

protocol A formal description of message formats and the rules two computers must follow to exchange those messages. Protocols can describe low-level details of machine-to-machine interfaces (for example, the order in which bits and bytes are sent across a wire) or high-level exchanges between allocation programs (for example, the way in which two programs transfer a file across the Internet).

router A special-purpose dedicated computer that attaches to two or more networks and routes packets from one network to the other. In particular, an Internet gateway routes IP datagrams among the networks it connects. Gateways route packets to other gateways until they can be delivered to the final destination directly across one physical network.

server A computer that shares its resources, such as printers and files, with other computers on the network. An example of this is a Network Files System (NFS) server that shares its disk space with a workstation that does not have a disk drive of its own.

Telnet The Internet standard protocol for remote terminal connection service. Telnet allows a user at one site to interact with a remote time-sharing system at another site as if the user's terminal were connected directly to the remote computer.

UNIX An operating system developed by Bell Laboratories that supports multiuser and multitasking operations.

WAIS Wide Area Information Server: An Internet service for looking up specific information in Internet databases.

WAN Wide Area Network

WWW World Wide Web

Portions of this glossary are adapted from the author's book "God on the Internet," copyright © 1996 by Mark A. Kellner and published by IDG Books Worldwide. All rights reserved.

Appendix: Y2K Resources

Where no counsel is, the people fall: but in the multitude of counsellors there is safety.
—Proverbs 11:14 (KJV)

The purpose of this section is to give you a number of resources for information and products that can help you become fully informed about the Y2K situation, help meet the needs of your neighbors, and prepare your family for whatever happens. This information is provided for your education. No legal, financial, or medical advice is given, and no warranties are implied. Also, neither Harold Shaw Publishers nor this author necessarily endorses all of the opinions expressed by the publishers or originators of the Websites and other resources listed below.

Having said that, I end this look at the Y2K situation with—what else?—links to Internet Websites containing a variety of information. Some of these go further than others in presenting speculations about what will happen; advertising from firms selling food and other Y2K supplies supports some of these sites. But all of the sites listed are worth investigating, at least to get a broad spectrum of Y2K viewpoints. (Note that *http://* has been left off the site addresses.)

Government Y2K Sites:

U.S. Federal Government Gateway for Year 2000 Information Directories—www.itpolicy.gsa.gov/mks/yr2000/y2khome.htm
This site offers links to the main Federal directories covering the Y2K issue from a government-preparedness viewpoint.

Federal Deposit Insurance Corp. Year 2000 Site—www.fdic.gov/about/y2k/

This site, maintained by the federal agency that insures many bank accounts, is a good starting place for official information about financial preparation for Year 2000 situations. It also maintains links to other government Websites for agencies concerned with Year 2000 matters.

U.S. Senate Special Committee on the Year 2000 Technology Problem—www.senate.gov/y2k/

This panel, headed by Sen. Robert Bennett (R-Utah) and Sen. Christopher Dodd (D-Conn.) is a tremendous resource for information on overall progress by the government and by major industries in getting ready for the Year 2000.

Federal Aviation Administration Year 2000 site—www.faay2k.com/

If you're wondering about getting on an airplane to fly on January 1, 2000, this Website will offer interesting information, and, it is hoped, some reassurance.

DGIII of the European Commission Y2K Site—www.ispo.cec.be/y2keuro/year2000.htm.

Directorate General III of the European Commission handles industrial matters for the pan-European organization. The site has excellent links to EC reports and media sources on what will happen in Europe.

Media-related Sites

The amount of media attention given to the Year 2000 situation will only magnify as the date approaches.

Christian Broadcasting Network Year 2000 Pages—www.cbn.org/y2k/index.asp

Produced by CBN reporter Drew Parkhill, these pages summarize major news events involving the Y2K crisis and offer copious resource links for Christians concerned about the matter.

The New York Times Millennium Bug Index—www.nytimes.com/library/tech/reference/millennium-index.html

(Free registration required.) Perhaps the leading "newspaper of record" in the United States, the Times' articles on Year 2000 are authoritative, clear, and helpful.

Y2K News—www.y2knews.com/
Here is a private publication, in print and online, providing information on the Year 2000 situation. Copious research and links to other sites make this a "must" for those researching the issue. Constant, daily updates.

Non-Profit Organizations, Disaster Relief

American Red Cross Year 2000 Tips—www.redcross.org/disaster/safety/y2k.html
This site, maintained by the American Red Cross, offers some prudent suggestions for Y2K preparedness, although it is much more conservative than many observers, suggesting (as this book went to press) that one week's inventory of vital supplies should be sufficient.

The Salvation Army—www.salvationarmyusa.org
While this group's Website does not (at press time) contain Y2K specific information, the Army's participation in disaster relief extends back to 1900, and its officials are involved in national preparations for Y2K relief, if necessary.

Adventist Disaster and Relief Agency—www.adra.org/
I recall seeing ADRA teams working in St. Louis, Missouri, after the 1993 flood of the Mississippi River. This organization is global in its outreach to disaster victims.

Private Y2K Sites

There are hundreds, perhaps thousands, of private Websites linked to the Year 2000 crisis. Here are several:

Year 2000 Information Center—www.year2000.com/
This site, maintained by author Peter de Jaeger contains the computer consultant's writings and many useful links.

Millennium Information Services—www.2000is.com
This firm, to which author Mark Kellner is a consultant, works with businesses and institutions to survey and help remediate Y2K prob-

lems. They also provide speakers to address groups on the Year 2000 situation. Kellner's Website (www.kellner2000.com) also gives Y2K information.

Y2K Prepare—www.y2kprepare.com
This is the Website of Thomas L. Clark (mentioned in Chapter 1), a Christian in Chicago who is convinced that Y2K will result in global disaster. This has prompted him to offer food milling and storage information.

Subject Index

AD2000 & Beyond, 96
Airlines and Y2K, 74-80, 146-47
Amsterdam 2000, 94-96
Apocalypse, 15-16

Celebrate Jesus, 96-97
Children and Y2K preparations, 137-38
Churches,
    and Y2K problems, 104-6
    and ministry, 106-7, 113-21, 135-39, 148-50
Computers
    advent of personal computers, 28-29, 35-37
    brief history of, 29-33
    first bug, 31
    Year 2000 problem, reason for, 33-35, 38-39

Debt Relief, 99-101

Elderly people and Y2K, 138-39
Embedded systems, problems of, 37-38, 104-6
End times predictions, 16-17, 43-44

FAA response to Y2K, 75-78
FEMA recommendations, 128-31

Finances
    and Y2K, 60-63, 66
    precautions to take, 63-66
Food storage, 126-27

Highway transportation and Y2K, 80-82
Home
    electronic systems and Y2K, 111-12
    preparations, 125-32

Insurance and Y2K, 66-69

Jubilee 2000, 93-94, 99-101

Lutheran Church 3-10 Campaign, 97-98

Millennium Bug
    causes of, 18-19, 33-35
    cost to fix, 21-23, 40-41
    local concerns, 51-53
    potential types of problems, 46-47
    when problems may begin, 45-46
    worldwide impact, 49-51, 144-46
Ministry opportunities, 25-26, 92-101, 113-21, 135-39, 148-50
Mission America, 96-97

Salvation Army Millennial Congress, 98
Stock market and Y2K, 66-69

Trains and Y2K, 82-83
Transportation and Y2K, 71-84

Websites for updates, 147, 155-58
Water storage, 125-26
Workplace strategies and Y2K, 108-110
Worst case scenarios, 19-20, 44-45